Who's Who in Thomas Hardy

Who's Who
in Thomas Hardy

GLENDA LEEMING

TAPLINGER PUBLISHING COMPANY
NEW YORK

First published in the United States in 1975 by
TAPLINGER PUBLISHING CO., INC.
New York, New York

Copyright © 1975 by Glenda Leeming
All rights reserved
Printed in Great Britain

Library of Congress Catalog Card Number: 74-24527
ISBN 0-8008-8271-7

Contents

Contents

Foreword

I can think of few novelists to whose work such a character-guide as this is so necessary a companion as Thomas Hardy. Anyone who is at all familiar with his major books will be able to recall the names of their protagonists, and probably of some characters who may be incidental, but who stand out by virtue of some graphically described eccentricity of appearance, speech or behaviour. Thinking of *Far From the Madding Crowd*, one immediately remembers Bathsheba Everdene, Gabriel Oak and Sergeant Troy, and perhaps Joseph Poorgrass or Matthew Moon. But who else? Yet I discover from Glenda Leeming's complete cast list that there are fifty-two people in the book. The number of characters Hardy created is enormous in proportion to the fourteen novels he wrote. Concise, readily accessible information about the lesser-known novels, such as *A Pair of Blue Eyes*, *The Laodicean* and *Two on a Tower* is even more valuable.

This is principally an exhaustive and clearly planned work of reference, and any student, teacher, or commentator on Hardy will find it an aid to the fallible memory, and, consequently, a fine time-saver. If I had had recourse to it, at school and university while preparing essays, I should have been spared endless fumbling through the novels to check essential, but elusive factual details. Can *you* unhesitatingly place all those 'minor rustics' in their exact contexts, or bring to mind Sergeant Troy's pseudonym, or remember just how many children Mrs. Leaf had?

But if the book is useful, it is also a delightful and unusual companion to Hardy's novels. He is, *par excellence*, a writer for all seasons and many moods; one re-reads *Jude the Obscure* or *The Mayor of Casterbridge* when prepared for serious intellectual and emotional involvement, and, say, *Under the Greenwood Tree*, for more light-hearted pastoral relief. Sometimes, I read only one particular chapter, or a memorable dramatic incident. But often, I want to immerse myself in Hardy's whole world, and do not have much time to spare. This book will fill a great need then. Browsing through it, I come across entries for innumerable people I had forgotten about, and realise again just how richly inventive and shrewd he is over the very difficult business of names—they all fit like gloves. And how beautifully he places a character with a single, uniquely apposite sentence of description. I looked up Mrs. Leaf (who had twelve children), to be reminded that she was to be seen each morning with 'her eyes mooning out through the panes of glass like a pot-sick winder-flower'. Glenda Leeming has a genius for extracting such quotations, and her own summaries of the characters are pithy and accurate. She has taken great pains, but wears her learning lightly.

Really dedicated Hardyeans can use the book for playing some joyous literary parlour-games. Which novel has the largest number of characters? How many members of the Chickerel family were there? Whose brothers required extra long coffins? What is Sue Brideshead's full name? And even, name some cows in *Tess of the D'Urbervilles*. (The answers are all in the text.)

Few people have space on their bookshelves for all the critical and scholarly volumes which accrete round the work of their favourite authors. But if you have Thomas Hardy's novels, and one good biography, you may well find that all the other books, apart from this one, become redundant.

SUSAN HILL

A

ADA: The girl who cleans the school for Sue Phillotson (*née* Brideshead) and makes her tea. *Jude the Obscure*

ALDCLYFFE, CAPTAIN GERALD FELLCOURT: A retired naval officer, Miss Aldclyffe's father, formerly Captain Bradleigh, as he is known when he befriends Ambrose Graye. Changes his name to Aldclyffe as a condition of an inheritance from his wife's family. Does not get on with his daughter. Dies the first evening Cytherea Graye spends at their home. *Desperate Remedies*

ALDCLYFFE, MISS CYTHEREA: Originally Miss Bradleigh, her family changing its name on coming into a fortune. At seventeen she has been seduced by a dashing soldier cousin, later killed abroad, and puts out her illegitimate son Aeneas with a widow, Mrs. Manston, visiting the baby sometimes under the name of Jane Taylor. Falls in love with Ambrose Graye but feels she must never marry, even though courted as an heiress. Cannot resist following Aeneas's career, and later, finding it is Graye's daughter Cytherea she has employed first as maid then as companion, she plans to employ Manston as steward and marry him to Cytherea. Foiled at first by Cytherea's love for Springrove, and Manston's secret marriage, later when his wife dies in a fire she blackmails Springrove into renouncing Cytherea, bribes her with promises of help for her sick brother Owen, only to have the wedding ceremony crowned with the news that Manston's first wife survived the fire. Ill and disillusioned, she only learns later that this surviving wife he produces is an impostor, and still believing his story of accidentally killing

I

his real wife, she continues to assist him until, being arrested, he commits suicide and leaves a confession of murder. She dies, begging Cytherea's forgiveness. Always peremptory and autocratic in character, her will being irresistible—'you might as well try to stop a footpath as stop her'—she is also good looking in middle age in a queenly, statuesque way, but her insistence on her own way causes more tragedy than her beauty has done. *Desperate Remedies*

ALDRITCH, DR.: Surgeon of Casterbridge who examines the murdered Sergeant Troy. *Far from the Madding Crowd*

ANKTELLS: An ancient family which has decayed from nobility to obscurity, like the Durbeyfields. *Tess of the D'Urbervilles*

ANN: The Swancourts' housemaid. *A Pair of Blue Eyes*

The little maidservant who works for Clym and Eustacia Yeobright. *The Return of the Native*

ANNY: Arabella Donn's girlhood friend, one of two who witness her meeting with Jude and advise her how to trap him into marriage by becoming pregnant. Meets Arabella again by chance at an agricultural show and after Arabella's widowhood they share a house together at Alfredston, and both take to the consolations of religion, Anny having been jilted by her young man. She continues to relay news of Wessex to Arabella who moves away. *Jude the Obscure*

ATWAY, MRS.: A Portland islander called in vain by Avice Pierston when trapped by a rock crevice. *The Well-Beloved*

B

BAKER, FARMER: An old friend of Farmer Springrove, converses with him on the topic of mortality on seeing a coffin they later hear is Manston's. *Desperate Remedies*

BALL, CAIN: So misnamed by his misguided mother who being ill-educated thinks Abel killed Cain, and though the parson corrects the error, the name is retained by the neighbours, who nevertheless soften it to 'Cainey'. *Far from the Madding Crowd*

BARKER, DR.: A young doctor of Budmouth who sees Sergeant Troy being swept out to sea while swimming, and assumes him dead. *Far from the Madding Crowd*

BARRET, SAM: Known for dragging his wife in a wheelchair round the church tower when she goes to be churched. *The Woodlanders*

BATES, GRAMMER: A deaf old lady of Endelstow. *A Pair of Blue Eyes*

BATH, DR.: A councillor of Casterbridge. *The Mayor of Casterbridge*

BATH, MRS.: A newcomer to Casterbridge through her marriage to the doctor, sits with Lucetta Farfrae at the royal visit. *The Mayor of Casterbridge*

BAXBY, LORD: Of Sherton; a family connection of Fitzpiers's mother. *The Woodlanders*

BEACH, ESTHER: A neighbour of Miller Loveday. *The Trumpet Major*

BEAUCOCK, FRED: Once a very promising lawyer's clerk and local dandy, but later loses his job through excessive drinking, and lives by giving legal advice for astonishingly small sums. He suggests to Mr. Melbury that his daughter Grace may be able to divorce Fitzpiers under the new divorce law, but probably from ignorance rather than duplicity his advice is unsound. *The Woodlanders*

BECKY: Avice Pierston's servant. *The Well-Beloved*

BELINDA: A neighbour of Miss Fawley at Marygreen, with whom she gossips. May be Anny's relation. *Jude the Obscure*

Lives at Marygreen. Through her, Anny her relation

obtains news of Marygreen, including Sue Brideshead's remarriage to Phillotson, to pass on to her old friend Arabella Cartlett (*née* Donn). May be Miss Fawley's neighbour. *Jude the Obscure*

BELL, BARBARA: An actress of about five and thirty. Is engaged by Paula Power to be her substitute in an amateur performance of *Love's Labour's Lost*. Miss Bell's fees rise by leaps and bounds as Paula's anxiety to engage her becomes apparent. *A Laodicean*

BELMAINE, MISS: A young lady who sings the different settings of one of Ethelberta Petherwin's poems. *The Hand of Ethelberta*

BELMAINE, MRS.: A lady sprung from a good, old family, of well-known courtesy based on real sensitivity to others' feelings. Is friendly with Ethelberta Petherwin. *The Hand of Ethelberta*

BENCOMBE, MARCIA: Daughter of the richest stone-merchant on the Portland peninsula, who as a wilful, tall, dark, imperious girl leaves home in a fury at being scolded for extravagance, and asks Jocelyn Pierston to help her escape to London. Although newly engaged to Avice Caro, he does so, and finding his elusive ideal of beauty in Marcia, suggests they marry. While living together waiting to get a licence, they quarrel frequently and in spite of being compromised she leaves him and returns home. The family move to San Francisco where her father loses nearly all his money, and Marcia later marries Leverre, a widower from Jersey. Though her junior, he dies leaving her to bring up a stepson Henri on a small income. Ironically it is her stepson who elopes with Jocelyn's fiancée, the granddaughter of the fiancée from whom Marcia has tempted him forty years earlier. Meeting Jocelyn again because of this elopement, she nurses him through a sudden illness, and their marriage in old age is based on convenience. *The Well-Beloved*

BENCOMBE, MR.: Richest stone-merchant on the Portland

peninsula, owner of the Best-Bed Stone Company, sells it, realises a large fortune and retires to London. Because of old business enmity with the Pierstons, he encourages his wilful daughter Marcia to return home from her elopement with Jocelyn Pierston, and his primitive, traditional Portland view is that she need not marry Jocelyn unless pregnant. This is not so and the family moves to San Francisco where he loses nearly all his fortune in speculation. *The Well-Beloved*

BICKNELL, MISS: The Swancourt household assume that Elfride on the night of her elopement is staying with Miss Bicknell at Plymouth as she has often done before. *A Pair of Blue Eyes*

BILES, HEZEKIAH ('HEZZY'): A Welland villager and member of the choir. *Two on a Tower*

BILES AND WILLIS: A firm that employs Jude Fawley to carve stone tablets in a church. Sue Brideshead helps him with this, which causes offence as they are known to be living in sin. *Jude the Obscure*

BILLETT, DAIRYMAN: Humble descendant of the once powerful Billett family. *Tess of the D'Urbervilles*

BILLETTS, DRENKHARDS, GREYS, ST. QUINTINS, HARDYS and GOULDS: Some of the many old Wessex families that have declined like the Durbeyfields from greatness to obscurity. *Tess of the D'Urbervilles*

BILLY: Postman from Anglebury on the Tolchurch beat; accompanied and made drunk by Manston who wishes to acquire an incriminating letter from Springrove to Owen Graye. *Desperate Remedies*

BIRCH, MILLY: Paula Power's maid, incorruptible and devoted. *A Laodicean*

BLANDSBURY, SIR CYRIL AND LADY: Attend the Imperial Archaeological Association's meeting at Corvsgate Castle and later meet Ethelberta Petherwin at Lord Montclere's

5

party at Enckworth Court; a lively pair of persons, entertaining as actors and friendly as dogs. *The Hand of Ethelberta*

BLORE, SAMMY: A Welland villager, member of the church choir, owns a tuning fork which is nearly a note flatter than the parson's. *Two on a Tower*

BLOWBODY, MRS.: A lady who sits near Lucetta Farfrae at the royal visit. *The Mayor of Casterbridge*

BOBBY: The boy horseminder of the carter who delivers coals to Marygreen and tells Jude Fawley his hearsay impression of Christminster. *Jude the Obscure*

BOLDWOOD, MR.: Gentleman farmer of Little Weatherbury farm, of distinctly outlined Roman features, quiet and self-contained. At first he is considered a confirmed bachelor, until his neighbour Bathsheba Everdene thoughtlessly sends him a Valentine, which works on his imagination, upsets the even tenor of his life, and finally makes him fall in love with her. Taking nothing lightly, he sets his heart on marrying Bathsheba and she, conscience-stricken, is being slowly won over when she happens to fall in love equally unfortunately with the philandering Troy. Boldwood, stricken by despair, lets his farm go to ruin, and saves it only by appointing Gabriel Oak as bailiff. When Troy is reported dead he resumes his feverish courtship and Bathsheba reluctantly promises to marry him after seven years' widowhood. Foiled again by Troy's return, he shoots him, and gives himself up. The death sentence is commuted to imprisonment on grounds of insanity. His transformation from imperturbable calm to madness results from years of pent-up emotion—his calm is 'the perfect balance of enormous antagonistic forces' which, once disturbed, destroy his balance for ever. Appears briefly in *The Mayor of Casterbridge* as a young man. *Far from the Madding Crowd*

BOLLEN, FARMER: A friend of Mr. Melbury. *The Woodlanders*

BOLLENS, FARMER: A dull man, according to Crickett, who secretly marries Adelaide Hinton, thus terminating her engagement to the reluctant Edward Springrove. Though old enough to be her father he is rich enough to be ten fathers. *Desperate Remedies*

BOWER O' BLISS and FRECKLES: Two ladies who sport moral characters of various depths of shade according to their company. They frequent the low tavern where Jude Fawley drowns his disappointments. *Jude the Obscure*

BOWLES: One of the three first-class London draughtsmen whom Somerset engages to assist him regardless of expense in preparing his competition plans for restoring De Stancy Castle. Has no beard. *A Laodicean*

BOWMAN, JOSEPH: A member of the Mellstock choir, rather dull of hearing. *Under the Greenwood Tree*

BRADLEIGH, CAPTAIN: *see* Aldclyffe, Captain Gerald Fellcourt

BRADLEIGH, CYTHEREA: *see* Aldclyffe, Miss Cytherea

BREEVE, DR.: The chief organist at Melchester Cathedral, to whom Christopher Julian is deputy and eventually successor. *The Hand of Ethelberta*

BRETT, SERGEANT: A master-tailor in John Loveday's company. *The Trumpet Major*

BRIDESHEAD, MR.: Father of Sue Brideshead, quarrels with and separates from her mother. Starts as an artistic metal worker, and will not receive his daughter at home after her association with the now dead leader-writer. *Jude the Obscure*

BRIDESHEAD, SUE (SUSANNAH FLORENCE MARY): A slim, charming intelligent girl with nervous little face and vivacious dark eyes. Her parents live with her great-aunt Miss Fawley, who brings her up, until they quarrel and separate. At eighteen she forms a friendly intimacy with an undergraduate who encourages her in wide reading and later they live together but platonically in London, and Sue blames herself for hastening his death by this frustration. Has taught for two years in London and is an excellent teacher but goes to work illuminating religious tracts at the same time maintaining an intellectual paganism, which also contrasts with her sexual frigidity. Through her cousin Jude Fawley she meets Phillotson and becomes his pupil-teacher. Flirting and winning the admiration of both men, in remorse she agrees to marry Phillotson, hastily carrying this out in reaction to Jude's confession of his own marriage. However her physical revulsion to Phillotson is so extreme that she jumps out of her bedroom window to avoid him, and soon leaves him for Jude with whom she feels a great affinity. However she also refuses to become his mistress nor will marry him even after both are divorced, having a nervous horror of marriage, though for the sake of 'Father Time', Jude's son by his first marriage, they pretend to marry. Few believe this pretence; and, especially after she reluctantly becomes Jude's mistress and has two children, social disapproval forces the sensitive couple to a life of wandering poverty. As Jude is ailing, they seek lodgings in Christminster where Sue's pregnancy and unwise frankness about her lack of marital status prejudice land-ladies against them. In temporary rooms her depression is communicated to 'Father Time' who kills himself and her two other children. Sue has a miscarriage and sinks into religious melancholy. Blaming self-indulgence for the tragedy, she punishes herself by remarrying Phillotson. Endurance of life with him soon makes her a 'staid, worn woman' and her claim to have found peace is disbelieved. Her cousin Jude's faults of impulsiveness and recklessness are intensified in her, exposing her to misfortunes, all of which she feels the more keenly for her extreme sensitivity: she is too vulnerable for the wide arena into which her enquiring spirit and modern education carry her. *Jude the Obscure*

BRIGHTWALTON, THE HON. MRS.: An old lady of seventy, a friend of Jocelyn Pierston. She asks him to a dinner, where he becomes more attracted to Mrs. Pine-Avon. *The Well-Beloved*

BROOK, MR.: A rector who attends the Imperial Archaeological Association's meeting at Corvsgate Castle. *The Hand of Ethelberta*

BROOKS, MRS.: Owner of the lodging-house where Tess Durbeyfield, passing as the wife of Alec D'Urberville, stabs him to death. Mrs. Brooks discovers the crime when D'Urberville's blood soaks through his bedroom floor to stain her ceiling below. *Tess of the D'Urbervilles*

BROWN, ABRAHAM: A lodging-house keeper of Hoxton in London, an old white-haired man with the ruddiness which makes white hairs so pleasing. He lets a room to Eunice Manston before her death. Unable to make lodgings pay, he moves to his native Cornwall where he soon afterwards dies. *Desperate Remedies*

BROWN, ANDREW: First clarinet in Kingsbere church, a good man enough but rather screechy in his music; his friend Yeobright would take a turn playing in church while Andrew had a nap. *The Return of the Native*

BROWN, DAN: Leaves a little tub of Holland's gin buried 'under the scroff' in Miller Loveday's fuel house, in return for a little porker. *The Trumpet Major*

BROWN, MR.: He has 'taken acres first and last' but 'never let an inch' and is offended when Springrove confuses him with Mr. Abraham Brown who used to live in the same house and let lodgings. *Desperate Remedies*

BROWN, SQUIRE: One of his birds is poached by Charl, who is caught with it. *The Mayor of Casterbridge*

BROWN, SMITH and ROBINSON, DOCTORS: Their notes on Romans, Corinthians and Galatians, Ephesians and Philippians are prominent in Parson Swancourt's library. *A Pair of Blue Eyes*

BROWNJOHN: A yeoman volunteer, fellow-trooper with Festus Derriman who teases him with stories of the invading French during the false invasion alarm. *The Trumpet Major*

BROWNJOHN, MRS.: Mr. Penny's daughter, just having her fifth child, three having died. *Under the Greenwood Tree*

BROWNLET, BENJAMIN: A horse-dealer, attends Casterbridge market. *The Mayor of Casterbridge*

BROWNLEY: A farmer whose buildings, moved from the hollow and rebuilt on top of the hill, seem strange to Giles Winterborne, but are forgotten and uninteresting to the returning Grace Melbury. *The Woodlanders*

BUCK, SERGEANT: A trumpeter in John Loveday's company. *The Trumpet Major*

BUCKLE, FARMER: All his pigs have rheumatism because of the damp sty they have lived in as striplings. *A Pair of Blue Eyes*

BUCKLE, MRS.: Landlady of the Falcon in St. Launce's, at whose inn Elfride Swancourt changes her clothes for the elopement. *A Pair of Blue Eyes*

BULGE, MR.: A wine merchant, attends Casterbridge market. *The Mayor of Casterbridge*

BURDEN, SIMON: A very old man, once a soldier, who watches at the beacon at night, ready to fire it as a signal that Bonaparte's invading army is coming, and does so in fact upon a justifiable false alarm. Though active, he is 'bowed to that degree which almost reproaches a feeling observer for standing upright'. *The Trumpet Major*

BUTTERMEAD, LADY MABELLA: A warm-hearted emotional girl who laughs at the humorousness of being alive. Introduces Jocelyn Pierston to Nichola Pine-Avon. *The Well-Beloved*

BUZZFORD: A general dealer, who frequents the Three Mariners at Casterbridge. *The Mayor of Casterbridge*

C

CALLCOME, NAT: Dick Dewy's friend and best man, intends to marry Vashti Sniff. *Under the Greenwood Tree*

CAMPERTON, MAJOR: A major in Captain De Stancy's battery, is to take the 'heavy line' in an amateur performance of *Love's Labour's Lost*. *A Laodicean*

CAMPERTON, MRS.: A dapper little lady who has most of the labour of organising an amateur performance of *Love's Labour's Lost* for charity. She plays the spritely Rosaline, though 'rather too old for the part really'. Is a friend of George Somerset's father, to whom she appeals for costume designs, a task he delegates to his son. *A Laodicean*

CANNISTER, MARTIN: Sexton of Parson Swancourt's church, with shrewd small eyes and a wealth of double chin which compensates in some measure for his considerable poverty of nose. Fascinates the child Elfride Swancourt with apocryphal stories of digging up familiar bodies and skeletons. Later marries Unity, the Swancourts' maid, and becomes landlord of the Welcome Home Inn. *A Pair of Blue Eyes*

CANTLE, CHRISTIAN: Grandfer Cantle's youngest son, a faltering man with reedy hair, no shoulders and a great quantity of wrist and ankle beyond his clothes, and painfully circular eyes surrounded by concentric rings like targets, singular as a man whom no woman will marry. Disgracefully timid, he none the less is recklessly tempted to gamble away the money his employer Mrs. Yeobright is sending by him to her niece Thomasin, and dares not admit it afterwards. *The Return of the Native*

CANTLE, GRANDFER: An old man of about seventy who prides himself on his achievements as a soldier in the Napoleonic period and on his unflaggingly youthful merriment and readiness for song and dance. *The Return of the Native*

CARO, ANN AVICE: Daughter of Avice Caro, the perfect double of her mother in appearance, but inferior in education though more flirtatious, less frank and more seductive. Since her family's impoverishment she has become a laundress, and Jocelyn Pierston, who has been tempted away from her mother, finds his ideal of beauty for once remaining stubbornly fixed in her—ironically, for Ann Avice is as fickle as he, and for her part soon looks elsewhere. Indeed she is secretly married to Isaac Pierston, and to avoid the attractions of a soldier agrees to become Jocelyn's housekeeper in London. Reluctantly admits her marriage at length, and, sent home by him, has a baby. Reconciliation with Isaac is encouraged by Jocelyn's financing a stone-merchant's business for them. At first ill-treated by her husband until business success makes him indifferent to domestic incompatibility. Later widowed, she proposes that Jocelyn marry her daughter, and the shock of having this thwarted provokes a heart-attack that kills her. *The Well-Beloved*

CARO, AVICE: One of the many Caros of the Portland rock peninsula, her branch of the family being the 'roan-mare Caros'. Her widowed mother struggles to carry on the family stone-cutting business. Avice has been quite well educated. A 'nice' girl—attractive but, above all things, nice—with intelligent eyes, broad forehead and thoughtful carriage, she is perhaps too open and frank to hold the charm of mystery for her childhood friend Jocelyn Pierston, but he becomes engaged to her, though not quite finding in her the elusive irresistible ideal beauty that often attracts him to women. When this ideal beauty beckons him from another woman, Avice is deserted by him. She later marries her cousin Jim Caro, has three children, is widowed, loses all her money and dies. The inaccessibility of death lends her a tantalising quality she never has in life, and Jocelyn loves her memory when lost as never before. *The Well-Beloved*

CARO, JIM: A cousin of Avice Caro, marries her after she is jilted by Jocelyn Pierston. Hopes to restore the failing stone-merchant's business but overreaches himself and ends in ruin. *The Well-Beloved*

CARO, MRS.: Mother of Avice Caro, a widow who tries to carry on their family's failing stone-merchant's business. *The Well-Beloved*

CAROLINE: A neighbour of Miss Fawley at Marygreen, with whom she gossips. *Jude the Obscure*

A master-baker's fair-haired daughter, courted by Bob Loveday while he is trying to give up his former fiancée Anne Garland to his brother. Caroline turns out not to be as good tempered as she seems at first, and is jilted. *The Trumpet Major*

CARTLETT: A short, rather bloated man with a globular stomach and short legs, resembling a top on two pegs; a publican who likes his own wares. Bigamously marries Arabella Donn in Australia, and after a quarrel follows her to England wishing to marry her legally. Though he temporarily refuses after she divorces Jude Fawley, they finally marry, and he is a kind husband in his fashion, though leaving her not very well provided for when he dies. *Jude the Obscure*

CARTLETT, MRS. ARABELLA: *see* Donn, Arabella

CAWTREE, FARMER: He keeps the ciderhouse at Hintock, and is invited by Giles Winterborne to a party where his lack of gentility offends the Melburys. *The Woodlanders*

CECIL, MR.: Lady Constantine's solicitor. His clerk brings her the news that her husband's death was much later than at first reported. *Two on a Tower*

CHALKFIELD, DR.: Succeeds Henchard as Mayor of Caster-bridge. He dies suddenly and Farfrae is elected as his successor. *The Mayor of Casterbridge*

CHALLOW: A burly pig-killer with a husky voice. Because he arrives late Jude Fawley and Arabella have to kill their pig themselves. *Jude the Obscure*

CHAMPREAU: Courier and valet engaged by Abner Power for his tour on the Continent with his niece Paula Power. *A Laodicean*

CHANCERLY, MR.: Lady Petherwin's lawyer. *The Hand of Ethelberta*

CHANGLY, JACK: A friend of Timothy Fairway, whom he disconcerts by grinning through the church window at his wedding. *The Return of the Native*

CHANNELCLIFFE, COUNTESS OF: A woman with a good-natured manner verging on that oft-claimed feminine quality, humour. At her party Jocelyn Pierston meets Nichola Pine-Avon. *The Well-Beloved*

CHANNELCLIFFE, EARL OF: A friend of Jocelyn Pierston. *The Well-Beloved*

CHANT, MERCY: Daughter of Dr. Chant, an earnest and devout young lady but rather prudish not to say narrowly Protestant, who their parents hope will marry Angel Clare. Easily shocked at Angel's opinions, she later becomes engaged to his orthodox brother Cuthbert. *Tess of the D'Urbervilles*

CHAPMAN, NATHANIEL ('NAT'): A Welland villager and member of the choir, where his jauntiness in singing is thought not quite becoming. *Two on a Tower*

CHARL: An ex-poacher of Durnover who frequents the St.

Peter's Finger public house. A moving spirit in the mockery of Lucetta Farfrae and Henchard in the 'skimmity-ride' procession. *The Mayor of Casterbridge*

CHARLES: One of Miss Aldclyffe's servants. *Desperate Remedies*

A boy who carries books and a message for Mr. Maybold to Fancy Day. *Under the Greenwood Tree*

CHARLEY: Stable-lad to Captain Vye whose granddaughter Eustacia Vye is to him a 'lovely wonder'. Three years younger than she is, but not backward for his age, he asks to hold her bare hand half an hour as reward for letting her take his place as Turkish knight in the Christmas mumming play, thus bringing her together with her future husband Clym Yeobright. Charley cares for her when she leaves Clym and returns to her grandfather; he removes the pistols she thinks of killing herself with; and ironically to amuse her lights a bonfire, not knowing this is an agreed signal this time to bring her together with her lover Wildeve. Grief-stricken after her death, he is grateful when Clym gives him a lock of her hair. *The Return of the Native*

CHARMOND, MR.: Dead husband of Mrs. Charmond, twenty or thirty years older than she is, who makes his money in the iron trade in the north, then retires to Hintock. *The Woodlanders*

CHARMOND, MRS. FELICE: Widowed landowner of Hintock, who before her marriage has been an actress. Thinks of taking the refined Grace Melbury abroad as a companion but has second thoughts on seeing how Grace's beauty detracts from her own. Perhaps from boredom she renews her acquaintance with Dr. Edred Fitzpiers (who has married Grace), whom she once romantically met as a student. They become lovers and she tries to dismiss him as gossip is injuring both, but relents and nurses him when an accident and quarrel with his father-in-law leave him injured and alone. Her vanity has caused her to use false hair bought from a local girl Marty South, and Marty's betrayal of this to Fitzpiers, in an attempt to part the lovers, causes a quarrel later when they are abroad. He leaves her, possibly pregnant by then, just in time to avoid a scandal when she is shot dead by a South Carolina lover whom she has formerly treated badly. A woman who has smiled where she has not loved and loved where she has not married, her expertise in 'cross loves and crooked passions' is at last fatal. *The Woodlanders*

CHESTMAN, DR.: Treats Owen Graye variously for the mysterious ailment in his leg. *Desperate Remedies*

CHICKEREL, CORNELIA: Ethelberta Petherwin's elder sister, has no education and becomes a housemaid. With her other servant brother and sister, she is a key figure in keeping the secret that the socially celebrated Ethelberta is letting out part of her grand house to lodgers. Later Cornelia acts as Ethelberta's lady's-maid when they travel abroad. She marries one of two farmer brothers, her sister Gwendoline marrying the other; all four emigrate to Queensland. *The Hand of Ethelberta*

CHICKEREL, DAN: Ethelberta Petherwin's elder brother, a carpenter who has to narrow his capabilities to suit city ideas when he moves to London. Goes into partnership with his more forceful brother Sol. *The Hand of Ethelberta*

CHICKEREL, EMMELINE: Younger sister of Ethelberta, is of a transitional age between child and woman, does her best to control and teach the youngest children while they live concealed in Ethelberta's London attic. Later when Ethelberta marries Lord Mountclere, Emmeline acts as her reader for the epic poem she writes. *The Hand of Ethelberta*

CHICKEREL, ETHELBERTA: *see* Petherwin, Mrs. Ethelberta

CHICKEREL, GEORGINA: One of the youngest Chickerels, for the sake of whose education her sister Ethelberta secretly takes in lodgers; but meanwhile the children have to remain hidden in the attic, deprived of air and exercise. *The Hand of Ethelberta*

CHICKEREL, GWENDOLINE: Elder sister of Ethelberta Petherwin, a cook with little education, comes to work in her sister's mansion to conceal the fact she is providing for her family by taking in lodgers. A countrywoman who cannot cope with city sophistication or French cooking, she marries one of two farmer brothers, her sister Cornelia marrying the other, and all four emigrate to Queensland. *The Hand of Ethelberta*

CHICKEREL, JOSEPH (JOEY): The younger sharp-witted brother of Ethelberta Petherwin, who takes to his rôle as her page with alacrity, but is outwitted by the cunning lady's-maid Mrs. Menlove with whom he becomes infatuated, as she worms out of him the secret of Ethelberta's origins in the servant Chickerel family, and threatens to ruin her high social position by revealing this. After Ethelberta's marriage to Lord Mountclere, Joey acquires a classical education with amazing facility and in spite of his preference for pagan myths his parents hope he will enter the Church. *The Hand of Ethelberta*

CHICKEREL, MR. R.: Father of Ethelberta Petherwin and her nine brothers and sisters. He is the greatly valued butler of the Doncastles and keeps secret his relationship with Ethelberta when she marries into high society. A thin, thoughtful man with bluish-white hair, his faultless professional bearing is shattered by the news of Ethelberta's impending marriage to the vicious Lord Mountclere, and he hastens to prevent it, but in vain. Is later established by his daughter in a new villa in Sandbourne. *The Hand of Ethelberta*

CHICKEREL, MRS.: An interesting woman of five and forty, confined to bed by a spinal complaint. Has been nurse in a nobleman's household until her marriage and afterwards plays the part of mother to her ten children on the whole affectionately and well. Is responsible for the naming of

17

her daughters after heroines of romance, a taste evidently passed on to her daughter Ethelberta Petherwin. *The Hand of Ethelberta*

CHICKEREL, MYRTLE: One of the youngest Chickerels, with her sisters Emmeline and Georgina is kept hidden in her ambitious but poor sister Ethelberta's attic, until enough money is saved to provide for her future. *The Hand of Ethelberta*

CHICKEREL, PICOTEE: Ethelberta Petherwin's next youngest sister: an April-natured, pink-cheeked, bright-eyed girl who far from being as enterprising as her sister is always dependent on her. Following Ethelberta's footsteps however in becoming a pupil-teacher, she still refuses to rise socially by ignoring her servant sisters or workman brothers. The messenger to Christopher Julian with a volume of Ethelberta's poems, she falls in love with him, and suffers to see him attached to Ethelberta, but after her sister marries Lord Mountclere, Christopher, aided by Picotee's growing resemblance to Ethelberta, comes to love her instead. *The Hand of Ethelberta*

CHICKEREL, SOL: Elder brother of Ethelberta, a carpenter of strong character and republican convictions, which appear both in his determination not to associate with his grander sister publicly, and in his objection to her marrying Lord Mountclere, the scion of a worn-out and doomed nobility. His knowledge of Mountclere's vicious reputation makes him hurry to prevent the wedding, but in vain, whereupon he refuses to help the newly enlightened Ethelberta to leave her husband, once married. Later allows her to help him set up in business with his brother Dan, strictly on the understanding that he will repay her. *The Hand of Ethelberta*

CHIMLEN, BILLY: A Mellstock choirboy, who has to be admonished not to 'sing quite so raving mad as you fain would'. *Under the Greenwood Tree*

CHINNY, JOSEPH: Porter at Carnford Road Station, a good-tempered, shallow-minded, ignorant man, who accompanies Eunice Manston to the inn. Later under the influence of illness and religious mania he reveals he has seen her leave the village alive after being supposed dead in a fire—thus making her husband's later remarriage to Cytherea Graye appear invalid. *Desperate Remedies*

CLARE, ANGEL: Youngest son of the Rev. James Clare, shocks his parents by his humanist rather than religious views, declining to become a clergyman. After spending years in different studies, his deep aversion to urban life excluding him from many professions, he decides on farming, and while learning dairy-practice at Talbothays falls in love with dairymaid Tess Durbeyfield. He persuades her against her better judgement to marry him, but when his confession of a former love affair with an older woman elicits her confession of an early seduction, he is horrified and leaves her to seek his fortune and forget his disappointment in Brazil. He provides Tess with an allowance but, though still horrified at her 'fall', invites one of Tess's fellow-dairymaids to go with him as his mistress: however he repents in time. His experiences and illness in Brazil reconcile him to Tess, but too late he returns to find her resentful, reproachful letter and eventually traces her to a hotel where, despairing of his return, she is living with her former seducer Alec D'Urberville. To his surprise Tess rejoins him outside the town declaring she has killed D'Urberville, and they finally enjoy a few days' happiness and mutual trust as fugitives before Tess is caught, tried and hanged. Angel then departs with Tess's young sister 'Liza-Lu, whom she has recommended him to marry, a 'spiritualised image of Tess' being likely to suit him better. For all his attempted independence Angel remains the slave of custom and conventionality when surprised back into his early teachings, and real maturity achieved by experience rather than theorising comes too late for Tess. *Tess of the D'Urbervilles*

CLARE, CUTHBERT: Second son of the Rev. James Clare, a

clergyman and fellow of a Cambridge college, the university world bounding his very limited horizon. Slightly more liberal-minded than his brother Felix, but with greater subtlety, he has less heart. *Tess of the D'Urbervilles*

CLARE, FELIX: Eldest son of the Rev. James Clare, a conventional clergyman and dutiful son, but more theoretically tolerant and practically censorious than his father. *Tess of the D'Urbervilles*

CLARE, MRS.: Second wife of the Rev. James Clare and mother of Felix, Cuthbert and Angel. A woman in cap and silver spectacles who can quote chapter and verse as well as her husband, and a devoted parish worker, she nevertheless cares nothing about Angel's heterodoxy as long as he returns safe home. *Tess of the D'Urbervilles*

CLARE, THE REV. JAMES: Clergyman of Emminster. By his first wife has a daughter, then by his second wife late in life has three sons so the youngest, Angel, is almost two generations divided from him. A clergyman of the old school of Apostolic simplicity and severity, he is nevertheless as kind-hearted and gentle as a child. Angel's humanism and farming ambitions are deeply painful to him, though he would welcome Angel's dairymaid wife. His enthusiasm temporarily converts the libertine Alec D'Urberville. *Tess of the D'Urbervilles*

CLARK, MARK: Works on Bathsheba Everdene's farm. A brisk young man, whom to meet anywhere on your travels was to know, to know was to drink with, and to drink with was, unfortunately, to pay for. *Far from the Madding Crowd*

CLAYDONFIELD, LORD: Of Chettlewood, whose agent Flooks has business with Manston. *Desperate Remedies*

CLÉMENTINE: The elderly French maid engaged by Paula Power, though not replacing Milly Birch. *A Laodicean*

COCKMAN: A handsome, dissipated young fellow who teases

Arabella Fawley (*née* Donn) when she is a barmaid. *Jude the Obscure*

COCKTON: One of the three first-rate London draughtsmen Somerset employs regardless of expense to assist him with his competition plans for restoring De Stancy Castle. *A Laodicean*

COGGAN, BOB: Small son of Jan Coggan; disgraces himself at the harvest supper by exploding with suppressed laughter during Joseph Poorgrass's song, and is sent home for his ill manners. *Far from the Madding Crowd*

COGGAN, CHARLOTTE: Jan Coggan's first wife, formerly dairymaid to old Farmer Everdene. She would never allow swearing nor the smallest item of talking in vain, and Jan wonders if this got her to heaven, 'But 'a was never much in luck's way, and perhaps 'a went downwards after all, poor soul.' *Far from the Madding Crowd*

COGGAN, JAN: Works on Bathsheba Everdene's farm and is a master shearer. A crimson man with a spacious countenance, and private glimmer in his eye. Popular and jovial, he is always the chief figure at local celebrations and ceremonies. Becomes Gabriel Oak's friend, gives him lodgings and is true as steel all through Gabriel's unhappiness about Bathsheba. *Far from the Madding Crowd*

COGGAN, MRS.: A wholesome-looking lady, who can toss a pancake or twirl a mop with the accuracy of pure mathematics. Works in Bathsheba Everdene's farmhouse. *Far from the Madding Crowd*

COGGAN, TEDDY: One of the many Coggans, a child who always has a loosened tooth or cut finger to show to particular friends. *Far from the Madding Crowd*

COMFORT, JAMES: A neighbour of Miller Loveday, serves in the Volunteers. A soldier by courtesy but a blacksmith by rights. *The Trumpet Major*

COMFORT, MRS.: A neighbour of Miller Loveday, probably the wife of James Comfort. *The Trumpet Major*

CONEY, CHRISTOPHER: An old man who works for Henchard; digs up the pennies that have been used to close the dead Susan Henchard's eyes and spends them on beer. *The Mayor of Casterbridge*

CONSTANTINE, LADY (VIVIETTE): While a beautiful woman of eight or nine and twenty, with hair and eyes of midnight black and a rich complexion, she is left alone by her husband Sir Blount whose passion for big-game hunting outweighs his jealousy. Her haughty and unwise promise never to mingle in society leaves her bored and lonely, and she falls in love with the beautiful youth Swithin St. Cleeve, some ten years her junior, though he is totally absorbed in astronomy. Her eagerness to help his studies in the observatory on a tower in her grounds, as well as the news of her widowhood, causes local gossip which eventually penetrates Swithin's absorption and awakens his love for her. They agree that marriage would end distractions from his work, though this must be secret because of their differing ages and social positions. Harassed by her brother Louis Glanville's promotion of the rich Bishop of Melstock's suit, and staggered by the news that Sir Blount's death was in fact later than her secret marriage, which is therefore invalid, Lady Constantine is checked in her haste to marry Swithin properly by learning that he has renounced a large legacy conditional on his being single. She renounces him, only to discover she is pregnant just after Swithin leaves for South Africa, so she hastily marries the bishop and passes off the baby as his seven-months child. Widowed a second time, she has unfortunately aged so much by the age of thirty-three that the returning Swithin is visibly disappointed. The shock of his heroic proposal to marry her nevertheless is too much for her weak heart and she dies. *Two on a Tower*

CONSTANTINE, SIR BLOUNT: Husband of Lady Constantine; his jealousy vies with his mania for big-game hunting until the latter wins and he leaves for Africa, warning his wife however to behave soberly in society, and when she haughtily offers to eschew society altogether, he takes up her promise. He later settles down with an African princess and though falsely reported dead does not die until after his wife's remarriage, which is therefore invalid. Leaves her little but debts. *Two on a Tower*

COOLE, MR.: A coroner, who is dining with Dr. Granston and accompanies him to identify Mrs. Jethway's body. *A Pair of Blue Eyes*

CORMICK, JIM: Son of old James, fellow-sailor with Bob Loveday; calls on the Lovedays to describe the Trafalgar action but unwittingly shocks Anne Garland by mentioning Bob's courting of another woman. *The Trumpet Major*

CORMICK, OLD JAMES: An old man, too dim-sighted to use his telescope, so that Anne Garland describes to him the flagship *Victory* on which his son Jim and her fiancé Bob Loveday are sailing. He owns the small boat that ferries Anne back to land from Portland Bill. *The Trumpet Major*

COX, MRS.: Dr. Fitzpiers's landlady, a retired farmer's wife, who is soured by her profitable lodger's marrying and moving away, and so passes on gossip that he has lowered himself by marrying Grace Melbury. *The Woodlanders*

CREEDLE, ROBERT: An old man who works for Giles Winterborne as he had for Giles's father, doing everything from making his bed to catching the moles in his garden, but his rough and ready housekeeping spoils the refinement of Giles's party. *The Woodlanders*

CRICK, MRS. CHRISTIANA: Wife of the dairyman Crick. A 'kindly, jolly sort of body', but mindful of social distinctions, so that she seats the gentleman trainee-dairyman Angel Clare apart from the other workers, and herself wears a hot, stuff gown in warm weather because the dairymaids wear thin printed cotton. *Tess of the D'Urbervilles*

CRICK, RICHARD (DICK): Head dairyman at Talbothays dairy, whose status is only visible on holidays as he works hard among the cows himself at other times. A kindly, stolid, unimaginative man. *Tess of the D'Urbervilles*

CRICKETT, MRS.: Wife of the clerk, a fine-framed, scandal-loving, formidable and much-married woman, with a peculiar corner to her eye enabling her to see behind her. Acts as temporary charwoman to Manston, and, discovering a long hair under his pillow, deduces that he is married. *Desperate Remedies*

CRICKETT, RICHARD: The parish clerk of Carriford, a 'kind of Bowdlerized rake', who eats only as much as a woman and has rheumatism in his left hand. Astonishes the neighbourhood by surviving his marriage to Mrs. Crickett, twice married before. *Desperate Remedies*

CRIPPLESTRAW, ANTHONY: A neighbour of Miller Loveday and member of the village Volunteer forces, though his toothlessness makes biting cartridges difficult. *The Trumpet Major*

CRUMPLER, MRS.: A heavy woman who for some reason dances in a clean apron at the Dewys' Christmas party. *Under the Greenwood Tree*

CRUMPLER, OLD SIMON: Too old to dance, sits by the chimney corner talking at the Dewys' Christmas party. *Under the Greenwood Tree*

CUNNINGHAM, CAPTAIN: Leader of the Longpuddle volunteers, sixty rank and file, mustered against Bonaparte's invading army. *The Trumpet Major*

CUXSOM, MOTHER: A good-natured gossip who frequents the Three Mariners; wears a purple apron, the waiststring so overhung by her sides as to be invisible. Her mother has raised the largest family of children in the parish. *The Mayor of Casterbridge*

D

DAMSON, SUKE: A hoydenish, fine-framed, bouncing young woman, who leads Dr. Fitzpiers on a midsummer's eve chase, at first though not later believing him to be her fiancé Tim Tangs. Is later seen leaving Fitzpiers's house at dawn, and his excuse that he has been performing emergency tooth extraction is discovered to be false by his bride Grace Melbury. Like Mrs. Charmond, Suke continues very attached to Fitzpiers so that after her marriage her husband Tim Tangs is jealous enough to set an iron man-trap for him. Her ambition is responsible for their emigration to New Zealand. *The Woodlanders*

DAN: Mr. Haylock's butcher-boy. *Under the Greenwood Tree*

DARCH, CAR: A tramping field worker, a dark virago, nicknamed the Queen of Spades. Once Alec D'Urberville's favourite, she is later jealous of his preference for Tess Durbeyfield. It is on escaping from Car's pugnacious attack on her that Tess unwisely accepts Alec's company. Car copes easily with the harsh work and conditions that tire Tess at Flintcombe Ash farm. *Tess of the D'Urbervilles*

DARCH, MRS: Mother of Car and Nancy; has a moustache. *Tess of the D'Urbervilles*

DARCH, NANCY: Sister of Car Darch, also a former mistress of Alec D'Urberville, nicknamed the Queen of Diamonds. Unites with her sister against Tess Durbeyfield, and works with her later at Flintcombe Ash farm where by preference they undertake men's work. *Tess of the D'Urbervilles*

DARE, WILLIAM: A boy-man whose appearance does not show whether he is sixteen or twenty-six. In fact the illegitimate son of Captain De Stancy, he appears first as a photographer and temporarily becomes assistant to George

Somerset, the architect hoping to restore De Stancy Castle. Dare's plan is for his father to marry their ancestral castle's present owner, the rich and beautiful Paula Power. Discovering Somerset is also Paula's suitor, Dare tries to remove him by betraying his competitive restoration plans to a rival architect Havill, but the plot fails when Havill, stricken by remorse, refuses his commission. Having persuaded De Stancy to abandon his vow of celibacy and pursue Paula, the resourceful Dare next forges Somerset's name to a demand for money, and falsifies a photograph to show him drunk. Thus discrediting Somerset, Dare is then threatened by Paula's shrewd uncle, Abner, who has supported De Stancy until discovering about Dare, whom he rightly suspects of intending to batten on Paula by blackmail in the future, but Dare bases counterthreats on his knowledge of Abner's disreputable past. Finally the marriage is prevented by the innocent Charlotte De Stancy's chance discovery of his plots, Paula's demand for his arrest and De Stancy's protection of him by revealing his paternity. Dare's lack of reputable family ties is reflected in his lack of responsibility: his farewell to De Stancy Castle is to set it on fire. *A Laodicean*

DARTON: A farmer whose name is marked on a Casterbridge market stall. *The Mayor of Casterbridge*

DAVID: Keeps house for Miller Loveday, and is very good at making the beds and dusting the legs of chairs and other furniture, though his sight is bad. Has worked there for thirty-eight years. *The Trumpet Major*

DAY, FANCY: Daughter of Geoffrey Day and his first wife. A beautiful young woman with rich curling brown hair and dark eyes. Brought up by an aunt who marries a rich lawyer, she is very well educated and takes the highest places in her qualifying examinations as a teacher. She retains, however, considerable vanity, absorbing interest in dress and an unquenchable desire for admiration. Her father, though well-to-do, wishes her to continue working as a schoolmistress so that her fortune will be as large as possible and will equip her to marry into a higher social sphere. She however comes to love Dick Dewy, who is of decent but not superior family. Her father's opposition to the match strengthens her attachment to him, and advised by a local wise woman she pretends to be pining away from thwarted love until her worried father consents to her marriage. Vanity makes one last dent in her loyalty when, overwhelmed by the temptation of social ascent, she agrees to marry the superior young vicar Mr. Maybold, only to withdraw her promise on better reflection. She never confesses this lapse to Dick and their marriage feast reflects the good old rustic traditions rather than her artificially acquired social elegance. *Under the Greenwood Tree*

DAY, GEOFFREY: Head gamekeeper, timber steward and general overlooker of the district to the Earl of Wessex. An unprepossessing man whose face is fissured rather than wrinkled, and whose nose has been 'thrown backwards' in a fight. He is known as 'a clever man if ever there was one. Never says anything: not he.' In fact he uses grim silence as a means of winkling information out of acquaintances. Proud of his daughter's refinement, he economises and wishes her to continue teaching, to accumulate a big enough fortune to fit her by wealth as well as education to marry above her station. However, when convinced that her love for the unremarkable Dick Dewy will, if disappointed, injure her health, he withdraws his refusal to let them marry. *Under the Greenwood Tree*

DAY, JOHN: Miss Aldclyffe's gardener. *Desperate Remedies*

DAY, KEEPER: May be Geoffrey Day, Fancy's father. His metheglin makes Joseph Poorgrass so drunk that he mistakes an owl's hooting for a human greeting. *Far from the Madding Crowd*

DAY, MRS. JANE: Second wife of Geoffrey Day, a woman in whom some eccentricities (indulged by her first husband and tolerated by Geoffrey) co-exist with common sense and

27

even a religious seriousness of tone on matters pertaining to her afflictions. Though plain and apparently doomed to spinsterhood, she has married twice, thus proving that 'Doom is nothing beside an elderly woman—quite a child in her hands'. *Under the Greenwood Tree*

DEBBYHOUSES: A family of humble carters, descended from the once powerful De Bayeux, as the Durbeyfields are descended from the D'Urbervilles. *Tess of the D'Urbervilles*

DERRIMAN, BENJAMIN (UNCLE BENJY): A miserly old squireen of skeletel appearance and nervous disposition. Formerly a tenant farmer, he now owns decrepit old Oxwell Hall where he has lived alone since the death of his wife and child. He goes to endless lengths to conciliate his big boisterous nephew Festus Derriman and conceal his money from him. Trusting Anne Garland above all his neighbours, he confides to her a map of the hiding place of his deed box, and briefly the box itself, which after some adventures turns up in Anne's chimney. Dying, he bequeaths most of his fortune to Anne. *The Trumpet Major*

DERRIMAN, FESTUS: Nephew but not, as he thinks, heir to Benjamin Derriman, he is at twenty-three a fine fellow as to feet and inches and of a remarkably warm tone in skin and hair, and moreover, 'his disposition dividing naturally into two, the boastful and the cantankerous', he is often fiery red with rage or hurt pride. Though cowardly as a rule, he can be tenacious once into a fight, and is a very nice fellow towards those who have the courage to ill-use him, though this does not include women: Anne Garland's mocking rejection of his advances drives him into a frenzy and he becomes quite vindictive. Characteristically his interest in Mathilda Johnson is aroused by mistaken belief that his former rival for Anne, John Loveday, is courting her, and he marries her in a spirit of vain competition. Failing to steal his uncle's strongbox, he is bequeathed only five small back-street houses. *The Trumpet Major*

DE STANCY, CAPTAIN WILLIAM: A man of nine and thirty, with sallow but interesting face and black moustache; son and heir of Sir William De Stancy, an impoverished baronet. Wearied by years in India, he keeps a vow never to indulge himself with wine or women, in penance for not having married a lady, now dead, by whom he has an illegitimate son. This son, William Dare, however wishes him to provide for them both by marrying the heiress Paula Power, present owner of their ancestral castle. He refuses until the sight of Paula at her gymnastic exercises rouses his latent spirit and decisiveness, but without success, as she favours the architect George Somerset. However, when his rival is rejected through Dare's unscrupulous tricks, and he inherits the baronetcy with his father's death, his persistence wins Paula's unenthusiastic consent. But just before their wedding, Dare's trickery is revealed, and to prevent Paula informing the police De Stancy confesses his paternity and is finally rejected by her. Honourable in his own conduct, De Stancy is ignorant of his son's machinations, but again honourably cannot abandon him to disgrace. *A Laodicean*

DE STANCY, CHARLOTTE: Descendant of the ancient De Stancy family, a rather short girl whose plain features are not improved by the inheritance of the 'family nose'; however her expression of tender affectionateness makes her almost pretty. Her character is fresh, childlike and thoroughly modern, and she has no regrets for her family's ancient riches and castle, now owned by the industrial heiress Paula Power. Her content is increased by the warm friendship developing between herself and Paula, until she unfortunately falls in love with Paula's suitor George Somerset. When her brother Captain De Stancy is about to marry Paula, Charlotte heroically reveals that Somerset has been tricked and misrepresented, thus breaking off her brother's wedding and ensuring that Paula will marry Somerset. She retires to an Anglican nunnery. *A Laodicean*

DE STANCY, CHIVALER: The original De Stancy, who

acquired the even more ancient castle and gave it his name. *A Laodicean*

DE STANCY, EDWARD: An ancestor of the De Stancys, living before the Civil Wars, portrayed with a mole on his face. *A Laodicean*

DE STANCY, SIR WILLIAM: Father of Captain De Stancy and Charlotte. In his youth has been recklessly extravagant, speculates his fortune away, and has to sell his family castle to strangers. After some years abroad he becomes ill, and the resulting slight softening of the brain removes his obsessive bitterness and intolerance for his lost heritage, so that he settles contentedly within sight of its walls, preaching an economy he has never practised. A very tall man even in old age, his gaunt features recall the stonework of his lost castle. *A Laodicean*

DEVERELL, MISS: A guest at Paula Power's garden party, a sallow lady with black twinkling eyes, a yellow dress and a gay laugh, who has no dancing partners. *A Laodicean*

DEWY, BESSY: Eight-year-old daughter of the Dewys, is bridesmaid at her brother Dick's marriage to Fancy Day. *Under the Greenwood Tree*

DEWY, BOB: Brother of Reuben, deplored by Mrs. Dewy as being a coarse-skinned, sweating man, as fat as a porpoise, who always addresses her with a low, mean 'Howst do, Anne'. *Under the Greenwood Tree*

DEWY, CHARLEY: Youngest of the Dewy children, four years old. Shows a childish propensity for getting covered in soot just at church time. *Under the Greenwood Tree*

DEWY, DICK: *see* Dewy, Richard

DEWY, JIMMY: Twelve-year-old brother of Dick Dewy, a treble in the church choir, who makes big strides like the men and does not lag behind with the other little boys. *Under the Greenwood Tree*

DEWY, MRS. ANN: Dick Dewy's mother, a good housewife,

who prides herself on coming from a refined family that 'kept itself up'; reproaches her robust husband Reuben for not keeping himself up likewise. *Under the Greenwood Tree*

DEWY, REUBEN: Tranter (irregular carrier) of Mellstock. A big ponderous man, he is often reproved by his wife in a marital way for being ungenteel and sweating so much. His slightly cynical nature makes him less enthusiastic and indignant than his fellow musicians at the abolishing of the old instrumental church choir, in which he plays first tenor violin, though as a capable, energetic organiser he is always their spokesman when they protest. *Under the Greenwood Tree*

DEWY, RICHARD (DICK): A young man of twenty with an ordinary shaped nose, an ordinary chin and ordinary shoulders. Falls in love with the new village schoolmistress Fancy Day and has to contend with obstacles such as her being better educated, more refined, richer and inclined to fickleness and coquetry. However, they become secretly engaged, Farmer Shiner's rivalry is thwarted, her father's reluctant consent gained, and they are married with traditional rustic celebration. Dick never knows that Fancy almost jilts him for the refined and socially superior Reverend Maybold, and though his personality is unformed it is his one effort to oppose Fancy's whims that establishes her respect and affection for him. *Under the Greenwood Tree*

DEWY, SUSAN: Elder daughter of the Dewys who at sixteen becomes Fancy Day's friend and eventually her bridesmaid. *Under the Greenwood Tree*

DEWY, WILLIAM: Father of Reuben, 'Grandfather William' to the Dewy family. A hale, active man of about seventy. His is a humorous and kindly nature, not unmixed with a frequent melancholy. However his exceptional religious and musical interests—he plays the bass-viol in the church choir —make him ever and instinctively come to the fore to arbitrate on these subjects. To his ruling passions his son adds 'cleaving up old dead apple-tree wood'. Like his grandson Dick, William's character is otherwise unobtrusive and generally ignored by the neighbours. Is remembered after his death in *Tess of the D'Urbervilles* as pacifying an angry bull with carols played on his violin. *Under the Greenwood Tree*

DICKSON, MR.: A talkative bachelor friend of Manston, he is surprised to be invited to stay with Manston, whose real motive is to use him as a witness of the arrival of a letter of contrition from his wife. *Desperate Remedies*

DODMAN, DAIRYMAN: An onlooker and wellwisher at Edward Springrove's marriage to Cytherea Graye. *Desperate Remedies*

DOLLERY, MRS.: A carrier with a van that takes goods and passengers. She wears leggings under her gown especially in windy weather, for modesty's sake; and a felt hat tied down with a handkerchief to guard against the earache. *The Woodlanders*

DOLLOP, JACK: A 'slack-twisted, 'hore's-bird of a fellow' who used to be a milker at Talbothays dairy, and being pursued by the mother of his pregnant sweetheart, hides in the big butter-churn, where she finds him and churns him until he promises to marry the girl. However he later marries a widow for her little income, only to find she forfeits it on marrying. *Tess of the D'Urbervilles*

DONCASTLE, MR. JOHN: Uncle of Alfred Neigh, the admirer of the dashing society lady Ethelberta Petherwin. He does not know that his butler Chickerel is Ethelberta's father, and when this is revealed he is appreciative rather than shocked. *The Hand of Ethelberta*

DONCASTLE, MRS. MARGARET: A friend of Ethelberta Petherwin who, unlike her husband, is shocked and affronted to learn that her butler Chickerel is Ethelberta's father. *The Hand of Ethelberta*

DONN, ARABELLA: A fine, dark-eyed girl when young, not

exactly handsome but well enough, though coarse in skin. With her rich complexion and fine figure she is a complete and substantial female animal—no more, no less. Enjoys working as a barmaid but is at home helping her father, a pig breeder, when she seduces Jude Fawley from his scholastic ambitions. She hopes to become pregnant so that he will marry her, a scheme that succeeds although she is (honestly) mistaken about the pregnancy. They quarrel and Arabella leaves him to emigrate with her parents to Australia, where she has Jude's child 'Little Father Time'. Him she farms out with her parents while bigamously marrying Cartlett, later quarrelling with him too and returning to England, but when she meets Jude again, Cartlett has followed her and, far from reconciliation, her aim is divorce to legalise the marriage with Cartlett. She confides Little Father Time to Jude and Sue Brideshead who are now lovers. Later widowed, her consolation in religion is short-lived as she is still attracted to Jude, and after Father Time kills himself and Sue's children, so that Sue leaves Jude to remarry her first husband, Arabella takes advantage of Jude's bitterness, makes him drunk, and marries him again. She feels cheated when she discovers his chronic ill-health, and though nursing him resignedly does not scruple to join in local festivities while he is on the point of death. With an eye to the main chance she has already marked down the 'doctor' Physician Vilbert as her next husband. Though coarse and unimaginative, she perceives (and despises) the self-tormenting sensitivity of her antithesis, Sue Brideshead. *Jude the Obscure*

DONN, MR.: A pig breeder and Arabella's father, originally an energetic black-whiskered man. Emigrates to Australia with his family, later returning to England, where he opens a small and precarious porkshop in Christminster. Here a long drinking party has the double effect of getting his daughter a husband and launching his porkshop into notoriety. *Jude the Obscure*

DONN, MRS.: Wife of Mr. Donn, Arabella's stepmother, a

simple, quiet woman without features or character. Emigrates with her family to Australia where she dies of dysentery. *Jude the Obscure*

DOWDEN, OLD: Olly Dowden's husband to whom, as he is sick, Wildeve promises to give a bottle of wine on his wedding day, which he does although the wedding has been delayed. *The Return of the Native*

DOWDEN, OLLY: A woman who lives by making heath brooms or besoms. Her nature is to be civil to enemies as well as to friends, and grateful to all the world for letting her remain alive; her simplicity makes up for her lack of tact and polish. *The Return of the Native*

DRAKE, JIM: A lad of Endelstow village. *A Pair of Blue Eyes*

DUMMETT, JOAN: Is took bad on the way home from Dame Ledlow's party, and is dropped by Jack Griggs in Dairyman Sweetapple's cow barton. *The Mayor of Casterbridge*

D'URBERVILLE, ALEC (ALEXANDER): Son of the rich Stokes, renamed 'Stoke-D'Urbervilles', no relation to the original old D'Urberville family. He has a swarthy complexion and full lips, and despite touches of barbarism in his contours his face has singular force. It is through his attraction to Tess that she gains employment tending his blind mother's poultry, and either by persuasion or force he evenually seduces her, though unable to make her accept the position of his paid mistress. A notorious libertine, he threatens the Rev. Clare who reproves him, but these reproofs gradually make him an enthusiastic religious convert, and he is preaching by the roadside when the sight of Tess distracts him anew. Wishing to control this attraction, he offers to redeem his earlier seduction by marrying her, but learning she is married already, he abandons religion to pursue her, and by attentions to her penurious family and argument that her separated husband will never return, he wins Tess to live with him. His sneers eventually provoke her to stab him to death, but in life Tess's gentle

34

instinctive paganism is no match for his blend of ruthless barbarism and ruthless civilisation. *Tess of the D'Urbervilles*

D'URBERVILLE, BRIAN: An ancestor of Tess Durbeyfield, who attends a great council in the time of Edward II. *Tess of the D'Urbervilles*

D'URBERVILLE, MRS.: Mother of Alec, a rich, white-haired, blind widow of no more than sixty, with the mobile face frequent in those whose sight has deteriorated only gradually. Her irritation with her son conceals a resentful love; she is bitterly fond of him. Her hobby being fowl-keeping, she employs Tess Durbeyfield as poultry-minder at her son's suggestion, but knows nothing of the supposed D'Urberville family relationship between them. *Tess of the D'Urbervilles*

D'URBERVILLE, SIR PAGAN: Renowned knight who comes over with the Conqueror and founds the noble D'Urberville family. An aptly named ancestor of the Durbeyfields. *Tess of the D'Urbervilles*

D'URBERVILLE, TESS: *see* Durbeyfield, Tess

DURBEYFIELD, ABRAHAM: The Durbeyfields' third child, a reflective boy. *Tess of the D'Urbervilles*

DURBEYFIELD, HOPE: One of the Durbeyfields' youngest daughters. *Tess of the D'Urbervilles*

DURBERYFIELD, JOAN: Mother of Tess and six other children, once a dairymaid and still showing some of the beauty Tess inherits from her. A 'passionate lover of tune', Joan is romantic; mentally she is merely one more of the Durbeyfield children, and not the eldest. Her light-heartedness verges on irresponsibility, as the optimism that cushions her against catastrophe also stops her troubling to guard against mishaps. Thus she beautifies Tess before sending her to the rich D'Urbervilles, thinking only of the possible benefits of Tess's beauty, and not at all of its snares. Superstitious and attuned to ancient village customs, her morality tolerant rather than delicate, she is of a culture two centuries older than her Victorian daughter. *Tess of the D'Urbervilles*

DURBEYFIELD, JOHN (JACK): Father of Tess and six other children. A 'haggler', peddling objects round the countryside. His fecklessness and weakness for drink are aggravated by learning that he is the last of a decayed, once celebrated noble family. In him family pride becomes scorn for any kind of work, and a fitful concern for his reputation that sets him against Tess's illegitimate baby. Suffers from a fatty degeneration of the heart which abruptly kills him. *Tess of the D'Urbervilles*

DURBEYFIELD, 'LIZA-LU (ELIZA-LOUISA): Four years younger than her eldest sister Tess, two children born between them having died. A serious, gentle, sweet girl who, Tess says, 'has the best of me without the bad of me', and is in appearance 'a spiritualised image of Tess', with the same beautiful eyes. Tess hopes that after her own death Angel Clare will marry 'Liza-Lu. *Tess of the D'Urbervilles*

DURBEYFIELD, MODESTY: One of the Durbeyfields' youngest daughters. *Tess of the D'Urbervilles*

DURBEYFIELD, SORROW: Tess's illegitimate baby. When Jack Durbeyfield proudly forbids access to the vicar, Tess baptises the dying baby herself, but it is buried in unconsecrated ground. *Tess of the D'Urbervilles*

DURBEYFIELD, TESS: Eldest child of John and Joan Durbeyfield, a pretty girl with dark hair, a flower-like mouth and beautiful large eyes of mingled black, blue, grey and violet. A good scholar, she hopes to become a schoolteacher, but while still young and inexperienced is sent to the rich D'Urberville family (who are actually no relation to the Durbeyfields) where she is to be employed as poultry-keeper. Seduced by Alec D'Urberville, Tess at once returns home, too proud to accept his love-making or to tell him of the later birth of her illegitimate child, whom she christens

Sorrow before it dies. She goes to work at Talbothays dairy where her reputation is unknown, and there she attracts Angel Clare, a clergyman's son training to be a farmer, and though she has vowed never to marry, she eventually gives way to his urgent persuasions and they marry. Her confession of her earlier seduction appals him and he at once leaves her, going to seek his fortune and forget his disappointment in Brazil. The allowance he gives Tess is claimed by her improvident family and she has to return to farm-work. To her surprise she encounters Alec D'Urberville, now an enthusiastic convert to Evangelical religion and a roadside preacher. Her attractions are too much for his new convictions, and after offering to expiate the seduction by marrying her, he casts aside principles and scruples to try to win her from Clare. With her father's death and the homelessness of her family, Tess is persuaded at last to live with D'Urberville, believing Clare has abandoned her. Made apathetic and ignoring the body she has given up to D'Urberville, with Clare's sudden reappearance Tess also gives up all moral distinctions and, provoked by D'Urberville's sneers, stabs him to death, hurrying after Clare. Fugitives for a few nights, they are at last caught in Stonehenge, and Tess is taken away to trial and execution, recommending Clare to marry her sister 'Liza-Lu. Dogged by unfortunate chances, from the death of her family's horse while she drives it, to the loss of her conscientious written confession, sent to Clare, Tess herself has the 'reckless acquiescence in chance too apparent in the whole D'Urberville family', and therefore makes the worst of every opportunity. Her own sensitivity, wherever it comes from, merely intensifies the sufferings she has to bear and provokes her to more intemperate action. *Tess of the D'Urbervilles*

DURFORD, JOHN (JACK): A friend of Dick Dewy's, dies of consumption. Dick, in fulfilling a promise to be his coffin-bearer, misses Fancy Day's debut as church organist. *Under the Greenwood Tree*

E

EDLIN, MRS.: A widow of Marygreen, writes to Jude Fawley about the illness of his great-aunt, whom she nurses. As the only surviving link with Jude's childhood she is invited to his unsuccessful attempt at marrying Sue Brideshead, where she is disgusted at the conscience-searching of modern couples before marrying. Later helps nurse Jude when ailing, and attends Sue's remarriage to Phillotson which she vehemently discourages. Finally goes to Jude's funeral, still lamenting the self-imposed anxieties of the younger generation in contrast with her own heedless days. *Jude the Obscure*

EDLINS, THE: A family known to the Donns. *Jude the Obscure*

EGLOSKERRY, MR.: A very small bachelor man of St. Launce's, with money in the funds. *A Pair of Blue Eyes*

ELIZA: Chambermaid at the inn where Manston and Cytherea Graye go on their wedding night. *Desperate Remedies*

The Phillotsons' servant at Shaston. *Jude the Obscure*

ELIZABETH: A maidservant of the D'Urbervilles. *Tess of the D'Urbervilles*

ELLIS, MISS: Mrs. Charmond's maid, dismissed for secrecy's sake when Mrs. Charmond and Fitzpiers go abroad together. *The Woodlanders*

ENDORFIELD, MRS. ELIZABETH: Her reputation among her friends as a Deep Body and among the vulgar as a witch stems from her very great shrewdness, lonely house, red cloak, pointed chin and negligent church attendance.

She advises Fancy Day how to win her father's consent to marry Dick Dewy by pretending to pine away. *Under the Greenwood Tree*

ENOCH: Geoffrey Day's trapper, a job he loses after many years when put in the stocks for drunkenness, so that Geoffrey has to find a substitute. Refuses to attend Fancy Day's wedding, probably from resentment, though Geoffrey attributes this surliness to excessive sobriety. *Under the Greenwood Tree*

EVERDENE, BATHSHEBA: A beautiful black-haired independent young woman, well educated but 'too wild' to be a governess. While visiting her aunt she meets her first suitor, Gabriel Oak, whom she refuses. Her fortunes rise when she inherits the lease of a prosperous farm from a rich uncle, whereas Oak fails in his sheepfarming, so that when he chances to save her ricks from burning she can reward him with employment as her shepherd. Wilful and active she runs her farm herself, and on a quickly regretted impulse sends a Valentine to her solemn neighbour, Farmer Boldwood, attracting first his interest then his violent infatuation. Torn between her independence and sympathy for him, she is considering marrying him when suddenly she in her turn is bewitched by the practised love-making of Sergeant Troy and, provoked by jealousy, marries him. Troy's extravagance, gambling and ignorance of farming threatens their livelihood, so that when Bathsheba finds he is the father of her former servant Fanny Robin's child, her dissatisfaction turns to outrage and she is more relieved than sorry at the report that he is drowned. Too depressed to manage her farm any more, she makes Oak her bailiff, and is unable to resist Boldwood's renewed and feverish courtship. However, at Troy's sudden reappearance at a Christmas dance, when the maddened Boldwood shoots him, she can still summon the willpower to take care of his body. Never quite sure of her rejected suitor Gabriel Oak, who has always refused to flatter her, Bathsheba is panic-stricken to hear he intends to emigrate, and at last takes the first steps in arranging their marriage. Hers is 'an impulsive nature under a deliberative aspect' which inspires her unusual and bold enterprise of becoming a woman farmer. Thus she and Oak achieve that 'camaraderie occurring through the similarity of pursuits', rare between men and women, and which proves the basis of 'the only love which is strong as death'. *Far from the Madding Crowd*

EVERDENE, FARMER JAMES: Bathsheba Everdene's uncle who leaves her the lease of his farm when he dies because of his high opinion of her powers. A very fair, good-hearted man. Also appears as Henchard's kindest creditor in *The Mayor of Casterbridge*. *Far from the Madding Crowd*

EVERDENE, LEVI or JOHN: Bathsheba's father, a gentleman-tailor and town-dweller, who isn't much to look at but becomes a very celebrated bankrupt two or three times. His eccentricity is only to feel attached to his beautiful wife when she takes off her wedding ring and pretends to be unmarried. Later however he becomes very religious. He and his wife die when Bathsheba is a small child. *Far from the Madding Crowd*

F

FAIRWAY, TIMOTHY: A firm-standing man of middle age, who keeps each corner of his crescent-shaped mouth rigorously drawn back into his cheeks to repress mirthfulness. Cuts the neighbours' hair for nothing on a Sunday morning, generally leaving them rather bloodstained. *The Return of the Native*

FALL, MR.: A weather prophet, nicknamed 'Wide-oh'. He rightly foretells a bad harvest to Henchard, who disbelieves him, gambles on good crops, and is ruined. In *Tess of the*

D'Urbervilles he is remembered with regret for his powers over butter-churns. *The Mayor of Casterbridge*

FARFRAE, DONALD: A young Scot, in the corn trade. While on his way to emigrate to America, he happens to help Michael Henchard who takes a violent liking to him and insists he stay as manager of his corn business. Fair, slight and intelligent, he seems at times overwhelmed by Henchard's size and boisterous energy, but his cool rationality marks his independence, and he often opposes Henchard. His employer's jealousy causes a quarrel, he leaves and sets up as corn merchant himself, becoming the more successful as rivalry stings Henchard to rash competition and eventual ruin. At first attracted by Elizabeth Jane Newson, Henchard's quiet stepdaughter, Farfrae is fascinated by the volatile, rich Lucetta Templeman, not knowing that Henchard, having formerly compromised her, intends to marry her. Her secret marriage to Farfrae causes further jealousy. As Farfrae has been less warm in friendship with Henchard, so he is less concerned in their enmity, and perhaps not realising his tactlessness, employs Henchard as his journeyman. When he also achieves Henchard's former office as Mayor, a fight ensues in which he is almost killed. However Henchard is honourable enough to keep his early love affair with Lucetta from her husband: learning of it only after her death Farfrae finds consolation in now being safe from that threatening scandal. Drawn again to the sober-minded Elizabeth Jane, he marries her and prospers. For all his solemnity his emotions are moderate only, and thus he comes through all his troubles with the cool detachment Henchard lacks. *The Mayor of Casterbridge*

FARFRAE, MRS.: *see* Templeman, Lucetta

FAWLEY, JUDE: After the death of his father, his mother having earlier committed suicide, he is brought up by his crusty great-aunt. Admiration for his teacher Phillotson, as much as his rudimentary night-school education, inspires him with reverence for the university-town

Christminster, where Phillotson goes, and to enter a college there becomes the lasting obsession of his life. Having taught himself Latin and Greek while working as his aunt's baker's boy, he apprentices himself to a stone-mason, to save enough to finance his studentship. But soon the desires of the flesh in the shape of Arabella Donn distract him from study, and he marries her when she says she is pregnant—later proved a mistake. They quarrel, she emigrates with her parents, and Jude goes to Christminster as a stone-mason. There he finds his hopes are ill-founded but is consoled by meeting his clever, spirited cousin Sue Brideshead. To keep her in the neighbourhood, ironically Jude persuades her to become teaching assistant to Phillotson, who similarly has been unable to enter a college, and to whom she later unenthusiastically becomes engaged. As a married man Jude cannot compete, and learning this Sue, who has been secretly encouraging his affection, in revulsion marries Phillotson. However Jude now meets Arabella who wants her freedom to remarry, and when Sue leaves Phillotson they both get divorced—impoverishing themselves further —and live together. Jude catches Sue's fear of marriage and they remain unwed, although as well as sheltering Jude's child by Arabella, 'Little Father Time', they have two more children of their own. Social ostracism and ill-health diminish Jude's income, which he has to supplement by baking and selling ecclesiastically shaped gingerbread cakes, until the old obsession leads him back to Christminster, where the poor family are refused shelter: in a temporary lodging Father Time kills himself and the other two children. Jude is embittered but matured by this tragedy, and now begins to prosper in his trade, but Sue sinks into religious melancholy and leaves him to remarry Phillotson. Arabella, now widowed, recaptures Jude by making him drunk, only to see him waste away, a process he deliberately hastens by visiting Sue in pouring wet weather. He dies as the rest of Christminster plunges into its annual festival. Jude's visionary imagination both urges him towards an elusive goal and lures him aside from it with the attractions of women and drink; his sensitivity in recognising an ideal is great, but he has not the necessary ruthlessness towards himself or others to achieve it. *Jude the Obscure*

FAWLEY, MISS DRUSILLA: Great-aunt of Jude Fawley, brings him up after his father down in Mellstock is 'took with the shakings for death'. Though lamenting the burden he is, she does her best for him. She has also brought up his cousin Sue Brideshead, and warns both of them in vain of the ill-luck in marriage usual in their family. Ironically Jude and Sue, both married to others, become reconciled at her funeral. *Jude the Obscure*

FAWLEY, MRS. ARABELLA: *see* Donn, Arabella

FITLER, MRS.: Ostler's wife and chambermaid at Springrove's inn, shows Mrs. Eunice Manston to her room. *Desperate Remedies*

FITZPIERS, DR. EDRED: A finely formed, handsome man, his eyes dark and expressive, soft of feature with some lack of firmness about his mouth. He is of an old impoverished family and has refinement enough to attract the well-educated Grace Melbury, whom he marries only to feel slightly degraded by marrying a timber-merchant's daughter, though not scrupling to accept Mr. Melbury's money. He falls in love with the widowed landowner Mrs. Charmond, whom he once met by chance as a student, and their affair ruins his reputation and medical practice. Injured by a fall one dark night, he quarrels with his father-in-law without recognising him, and in a scuffle gains further injuries, for which Mrs. Charmond nurses him and they go abroad together. After they part in anger he seeks reconciliation with Grace, thwarted by her flight. Nonplussed by her assertion that she was Giles Winterborne's mistress before his death, Fitzpiers later decides this is untrue and with great patience persuades her at last to forgive him. Fortunately he inherits a legacy which makes him independent and they go to live in a distant part of England. Charming without being dandified, Fitzpiers has always had great intellectual ability threatened by lack of concentration, but his later more ascetic appearance after his sufferings suggest he has become more settled. *The Woodlanders*

FITZPIERS, MRS.: *see* Melbury, Grace

FLOOKS, MR.: Agent to Lord Claydonfield at Chettlewood. Important business with him prevents Manston meeting his wife at the station as arranged. *Desperate Remedies*

FLOWER, CAPTAIN: In his cottage at Knollsea Ethelberta Petherwin finds lodgings for herself and her younger sisters, exhausted by the strain and confinement of London society. An experienced sailor, with rich stentorian voice developed against high coastal winds for twenty years, he is adept and nimble in the kitchen too. The two great ventures of his life have been lost in the treacherous Knollsea Bay, leaving him poor and the coxwain of the very necessary local lifeboat. *The Hand of Ethelberta*

FLOY, MR.: Coroner at the enquiry into the supposed death of Eunice Manston. *Desperate Remedies*

FONTOVER, MISS: An elderly lady in spectacles, Sue Brideshead's employer and landlady, owner of an ecclesiastical artwork shop, and a 'Dab at Ritual', as becomes one of her business, which she has started on the death of her father, a clergyman. Discovering Sue has some casts of nude Greek statues in her room, she breaks them, and Sue leaves her house and employment. *Jude the Obscure*

FRANCES: A flaxen-haired, married dairywoman, who works at Talbothays dairy but lives in her own cottage, consumptive from the winter damps of the watermeads. *Tess of the D'Urbervilles*

FRANCIS, MR.: A pseudonym used by Sergeant Troy. *Far from the Madding Crowd*

FRAY, HENERY: Insists on the superfluous 'e' in his name.

Works on Bathsheba Everdene's farm. A man of more than middle age who lays it down that the law of the world is bad. Resentful against Bathsheba for not making him her bailiff, and later against Gabriel Oak who eventually gains that position. *Far from the Madding Crowd*

FRED: The thin, lath-like lad who takes a message for John Durbeyfield to the Pure Drop inn. *Tess of the D'Urbervilles*

FREDDY, LITTLE: A boy treble in the Welland choir. *Two on a Tower*

FRY, AMOS ('HAYMOSS'): A farm labourer whose clothes in the traditional way harmonise with the landscape. A member of the Welland choir. *Two on a Tower*

FYANDER, DEBORAH: A slovenly old dairywoman at Talbothays, who has to be admonished to wash her hands. *Tess of the D'Urbervilles*

G

GARLAND, ANNE: Only child of Mrs. Garland, a landscape painter's widow. Poetically fair, with brown curls, graceful and slender, she combines dignity with sweetness as no other girl can do. Lodging with her mother in part of Miller Loveday's mill, she considers herself superior to her admirer Trumpet Major John Loveday, the miller's earnest elder son, though superiority is forgotten when the younger son, her childhood sweetheart Bob, returns from sea. Affronted by his hasty engagement to Mathilda Johnson, Anne keeps him at a distance when he turns from the unworthy Mathilda to herself; but, flying to his protection from her importunate, rich, but ridiculous suitor Festus Derriman, she admits her love for him. Their engagement is ill-starred, as a narrow escape from the pressgang and contrition at finding he has ruined his brother's hopes decide Bob to renounce Anne for John and volunteer to sail against Bonaparte's invasionary forces. Though left without letters, Anne waits patiently until she hears of his engagement to a Portsmouth girl. Shocked and humiliated she is eventually impressed by John's fidelity and is beginning to encourage him when the fickle Bob withdraws his renunciation, and after further contrition and penitence is forgiven. Anne does not deserve to be passed like a parcel from brother to brother, for, a sensible girl of 'real firmness', she remains true to her early attachment, however unworthy, realising, as she tells John, that gratitude is not love. *The Trumpet Major*

GARLAND, MRS. MARTHA: Widow of a landscape painter, she is a woman of forty, with sanguine mouth and eye, unheroic manner and pleasant general appearance—a little more tarnished as to surface but not much worse in contour than her young daughter. Of a friendly, thankful nature, she relies much on her landlord Miller Loveday, part of whose mill house she rents for its cheapness since her husband's death, and though inhabiting a twilight rank between gentle and simple, superior to Loveday's, she eventually agrees to marry him. Her ambitions for Anne incline to a match with Festus Derriman the squire's nephew, but she allows her daughter her own way. *The Trumpet Major*

GEORGE: Menlove denies he is ever a lover of hers. *The Hand of Ethelberta*

One of Mrs. Yeobright's brothers, all so tall that they require extra long coffins, poor George's knees being crumpled up a little even so. *The Return of the Native*

GIBSEY, TED: One of Ann Avice Caro's admirers, who will help her with the heaviest laundry work if she lets him. *The Well-Beloved*

GILLINGHAM, GEORGE: Richard Phillotson's old college

friend, a cool, practical man who disapproves of Phillotson's allowing his wife to leave him for another man, and advises him to resign his job rather than provoke scandalous dismissal. Later gives Sue away when Phillotson remarries her. *Jude the Obscure*

GLANVILLE, LOUIS: Brother of Lady Constantine, a slightly built man of perhaps thirty, with small dark eyes. A restless unsettled sort of person, he never persists in anything and leaves his post as attaché at Rio de Janeiro to seek new prospects. Visits his sister and urges her to remarry a rich man, preferably the susceptible Bishop of Melstock, not knowing of her secret marriage to Swithin St. Cleeve. After foiling his suspicions, Lady Constantine finally confesses all to him, in despair because her remarriage has proved invalid and left her pregnant. As St. Cleeve is abroad, Louis acts boldly to arrange her hasty marriage to the bishop. *Two on a Tower*

GLIM, MR.: The curate Parson Swancourt can afford after marrying a rich widow. *A Pair of Blue Eyes*

GOODENOUGH, MRS.: The seller of furmity porridge, laced —at a price—with rum. Made drunk by her wares, Michael Henchard sells his wife Susan. Eighteen years later the furmity-seller and her wares have deteriorated greatly, but she tells Susan when Henchard lives; and later still, when summoned for drunkenness before Henchard as Magistrate, her recollection of his youthful rashness ruins his reputation. *The Mayor of Casterbridge*

GOODMAN, MRS.: An elderly lady, left in narrow circumstances, lives with her rich young niece Paula Power as chaperon and adviser—'in short as ballast to the management'. Favours Paula's suitor George Somerset. *A Laodicean*

GRADFIELD, MR.: A stout, grey-bearded burgher of sixty, and architect friend of Ambrose Graye who agrees to take on Ambrose's son Owen temporarily as assistant in his Budmouth Regis office. *Desperate Remedies*

GRANSON, DR.: The Swancourts' family doctor. *A Pair of Blue Eyes*

GRAYE, AMBROSE: An architect, whose life is blighted by his disappointed love for Cytherea Bradleigh (Aldclyffe). Broken-hearted by her unexpected rejection, though he later marries a lady fairly well endowed with money and good looks, he continues to repine after his lost Cytherea, his character deteriorating from its original receptiveness to a moody depression. This lackadaisical tendency leads to improvidence and professional mediocrity, and soon after his wife dies, though resolving to provide better for his children, he characteristically drifts into absentmindedness and falls to his death from a church-tower, leaving his children burdened by debt. *Desperate Remedies*

GRAYE, CYTHEREA: Daughter of Ambrose Graye, named after his lost love. Her curly hair is golden brown, her sapphire-blue eyes express good faith and loyalty, but her chief charm is her innate gracefulness. After her father's death she hopes to find work as a governess or companion instead of depending on her brother Owen, but finding no employer she at last is engaged by Miss Aldclyffe as lady's-maid. On the verge of dismissal because of her inexperience and her employer's temper she discovers Miss Aldclyffe is the same Cytherea Bradleigh her father once loved, and Miss Aldclyffe, discovering this likewise, promotes her to companion. Although she loves her brother's colleague Edward Springrove, his prior and regretted engagement to another, and Miss Aldclyffe's peremptory wish that her steward (really her illegitimate son) Aeneas Manston shall marry Cytherea, make her unhappy. Agreeing to marry Manston at last so that Miss Aldclyffe will help her brother, now seriously ill, Cytherea is saved on her wedding night by the news that Manston's first wife has not died in a fire, as supposed. Kept in suspense, neither free nor committed, and a subject of gossip, Cytherea is at last released by Manston's confession to murdering his first wife and his suicide. She then marries Springrove. A sensible and usually light-hearted girl, she is sensitive enough to become almost morbid under her strange fortunes. *Desperate Remedies*

GRAYE, OWEN: Son of Ambrose Graye. A rather dogmatic and unimaginative young man, he is sincerely fond of his sister. In place of his father's sensitivity he has a larger share of pride and a positive set of opinions that just miss prejudice. His anxiety to pay off his father's debts is thwarted by a sudden and serious disease of his leg, the incapacity and expense caused by this making him urge his unwilling sister Cytherea to marry Aeneas Manston, whose help, like the rich Miss Aldclyffe's assistance, is conditional on this marriage. His recovery of health is accompanied by professional success, so that he can support his sister when the eventual marriage turns out to be invalid. Aided by his former colleague Springrove, he investigates the truth about Manston's first wife, eventually finding Manston has murdered her. He celebrates a return to respectability with Cytherea's marriage to Springrove, where he 'prides away his hearing' of a humble acquaintance's greeting. Wins an architectural competition and moves to London. *Desperate Remedies*

GREEN, ANTHONY: Lady Constantine's one manservant, after her impoverishment. Formerly a poor day labourer, he is inclined to stay a bachelor, but marries Gloriana because of her pleas 'to stand by her and save her from unborn shame', and also because of pressure exerted by Lady Constantine. *Two on a Tower*

GREEN, LAWYER: A man as sharp as a needle; marries Fancy Day's schoolmistress aunt. *Under the Greenwood Tree*

GREEN, LITTLE JEMMY: A doctor, on the fringes of whose practice Dr. Fitzpiers sets up his own practice. *The Woodlanders*

GREEN, MRS. GLORIANA: Lady Constantine's woman servant, loyal to her mistress who has influenced Anthony to make an honest woman of her, after which she goes to live in the village with her husband and child. However, she accompanies Lady Constantine on a supposed holiday in Bath, but never learns of her mistress's secret wedding there, being recalled home suddenly to her sick child. *Two on a Tower*

GREY: An acquaintance of Neigh's, at whose house he first hears of Ethelberta Petherwin's romance performances. *The Hand of Ethelberta*

GRIGGS, JACK: Drops the suffering Joan Dummett in Dairyman Sweetapple's cow barton while carrying her home from a party. *The Mayor of Casterbridge*

GRIMMETT, JOHN: A Mellstock butcher, competitor to Mr. Haylock. *Under the Greenwood Tree*

GRINHAM, MR.: Mr. Maybold's predecessor as Vicar of Mellstock, fondly remembered for 'not putting a parish to unnecessary trouble'. His rough and ready ways appal Mr. Maybold. *Under the Greenwood Tree*

GROBY, FARMER: A well-to-do boor of Trantridge, tenant-farmer of Flintcombe Ash, whose comments on Tess Durbeyfield's seduction are overheard but disbelieved by Angel Clare, who knocks him down. In revenge for this Groby victimises Tess when she later comes to work on his farm, which she endures because though a bully he is not a libertine. *Tess of the D'Urbervilles*

GROWER, BENJAMIN: A prominent burgess of Casterbridge. He is a creditor of Henchard, who hopes to extend his credit by showing that the rich Lucetta Templeman is to marry him as she has promised, but she reveals that this is impossible, as she has by chance just asked Grower to witness her secret marriage to Farfrae. *The Mayor of Casterbridge*

GRUCHETTE, MISS: Lord Mountclere's mistress, she lives in an ornamental cottage in his park, ostensibly to tend the fowls, with two servants to wait on her. This is discovered by Ethelberta Petherwin who therefore, having just married Lord Mountclere, impulsively but unsuccessfully attempts to escape and bargain for better conduct. Miss Gruchette is said to be immovably established, but in fact is dismissed by Mountclere. *The Hand of Ethelberta*

H

HALWAY, MR.: The auctioneer who sells Eunice Manston's workbox to Mrs. Higgins. *Desperate Remedies*

HAMMER AND RAWLES: Solicitors to Swithin St. Cleeve's great-uncle Jocelyn St. Cleeve. They administer the bequest which is conditional on Swithin's remaining single. *Two on a Tower*

HANNAH: Old servant or assistant to old Mrs. Martin, who refers to her as a decrepit childish creature tolerated from charity, though Hannah is in fact younger and spryer than her mistress. Dies while Swithin St. Cleeve is in South Africa. *Two on a Tower*

HARRIS, OLD JIMMY: Blacksmith, whose distinctive make of horseshoe enables Oak and Coggan to track the missing horse Dainty. *Far from the Madding Crowd*

HARRY: An Egdon Heath boy who acts the Saracen in the Christmas mumming play and 'should strut a bit more'. *The Return of the Native*

HAVILL, JAMES: An architect of Toneborough, a bearded man with cold grey eyes, he is employed by the late Mr. Power to build a Baptist chapel and expects to restore De Stancy Castle. Its owner Paula Power however mistrusts him when his ignorance of authentic old styles is elicited by the tactless young architect George Somerset, but she is persuaded to let Havill and Somerset compete for the commission. Deep in debt, Havill is in despair until Somerset's unscrupulous assistant Dare betrays Somerset's designs to him, and newly inspired he submits plans that are judged equal to Somerset's. Sympathising with his distress and debt, Paula pays him in advance to execute a half-share of the restoration, but when his wife dies he is stricken by remorse and withdraws. Somerset is later slandered and dismissed, but Havill's re-engagement is disappointing, for Dare and De Stancy, the latter being engaged to marry Paula, limit and interfere with his work. Basically honest though without very high principles, he is last seen helping fight the fire that finally destroys the castle. *A Laodicean*

HAWES, MRS.: A widow with whom Sue Bridehead lodges while working as Phillotson's pupil-teacher. *Jude the Obscure*

HAYLOCK, MR.: Butcher of Mellstock, who serves the Day family and reports Fancy Day's alarmingly reduced meat order to her father. *Under the Greenwood Tree*

HAZE, CUNNINGHAM: A man with a grizzled beard and piercing eyes, Chief Constable of the district that includes De Stancy Castle. He has glimpsed Dare and Havill spying on Somerset's architectural plans and being able to recognise Dare again is a threat to him. *A Laodicean*

HELMSDALE, BISHOP CUTHBERT: Bishop of Mellstock, he is a bachelor of about fifty, who is earnest and well meaning but not without faults—these include arrogance. Perhaps also impulsive, he wishes to marry Lady Constantine, an idea fostered by her brother, but he is refused by her because of her secret marriage to St. Cleeve. However when she finds to her horror that she is pregnant and that her marriage is invalid, St. Cleeve being abroad, the bishop is unwittingly used as a solution to the problem, and, persuaded by her brother, proposes again and is accepted. The child is passed off as premature, but not unjustly their married life is not idyllic and he dies of a short illness at the comparatively early age of fifty-four. *Two on a Tower*

HENCHARD, ELIZABETH JANE: The real daughter of Michael Henchard dies in infancy, though her name is also given to her half-sister, Newson's daughter. *The Mayor of Casterbridge. See* Newson, Elizabeth Jane

HENCHARD, MICHAEL: A large-built, swarthy, high-coloured man, unrestrained in his loves and hates. As a young man he is given to occasional drinking bouts, during one of which he blames his early marriage for his poverty and offers to sell his wife and child for five guineas, an offer taken up by the sailor Newson. When sober, Henchard cannot trace them and can only express his repentance in a vow of abstinence from drink for twenty years. His wife Susan finds him again much later as prosperous corn dealer and Mayor of Casterbridge, and he 'remarries' her to provide for the child, Elizabeth Jane, only to find when Susan dies that his child has died long before and this Elizabeth Jane is Newson's daughter. His affection for her turns into dislike, and similarly his 'tigerish affection' for Donald Farfrae, a Scot he has pressed to become his manager, becomes tainted by jealousy and turns to violent hatred, even though he has confided in him secrets about the 'sale' of Susan, and also about having compromised a Jersey girl, Lucetta. Fuel is added to his hatred when Lucetta re-appears, now with a handsome inheritance, employs Elizabeth Jane as companion, and instead of accepting Henchard's belated offer of marriage, prefers Farfrae. Brutally Henchard blackmails her into promising marriage, but partly because his scandalous 'sale' of Susan now becomes public, she secretly marries Farfrae. This scandal, a disastrous harvest, and reckless competition with Farfrae ruin his business, which, with his house and furniture, are bought by Farfrae and Lucetta, and he becomes their employee. He overcomes the temptation to reveal his early association with Lucetta, but this is betrayed anyway by his acquaintance and landlord Jopp, the scandal directly causing Lucetta's death in childbirth. A broken man, Henchard is tended by Elizabeth Jane, who still thinks him her father, and comes to love her. When her real father Newson reappears, Henchard's false story of Elizabeth Jane's death is soon discovered; she rejects Henchard and marries Farfrae, given away by Newson. Henchard dies self-exiled to the bare countryside, demanding that his grave shall be unmarked and forgotten. A man of immense energy, he is his own worst enemy in that this energy can as easily turn to evil as to good, and he dies with a stoicism as thoroughgoing as his love or hate. *The Mayor of Casterbridge*

HENCHARD, MRS. SUSAN: Wife of Michael Henchard, who blames their early marriage for hindering his career. He becomes drunk at a fair and offers to sell her; bitterly she agrees that the sailor Newson shall 'buy' her and her child Elizabeth Jane for five guineas, believing in her ignorance that this is a legal contract. After many years with Newson she learns her mistake and is relieved when he is reported drowned. Seeking out Henchard she finds him rich and Mayor of Casterbridge. She leads him to believe her daughter by Newson, also called Elizabeth Jane, is his child, who in fact has died in infancy. They 'remarry', their earlier marriage being a secret even from Elizabeth Jane, though this causes surprise as Susan is now worn and frail. Weakened by her hard life she dies, and her deceit about Elizabeth Jane's parentage is discovered by Henchard. Without bloom or artifice of any kind she has handsome features which become beautiful in her less careworn daughter. Her intention is always to do right, though the circumstances of her life lead her astray. *The Mayor of Casterbridge*

HENGISTBURY, LORD: Grandfather of Nichola Pine-Avon. *The Well-Beloved*

HEWBY, WALTER: A London architect, Stephen Smith's employer. *A Pair of Blue Eyes*

HIGGINS, MRS.: The wife of a carpenter who from want of

employment one winter decides to marry, both later taking to drink. They have six or seven small children and provide a depressing picture of married life among the very poor of a city. She buys Eunice Manston's workbox in a mixed lot at an auction sale. *Desperate Remedies*

HIGHRIDGE, MR.: A young curate of Marygreen, who takes a keen interest in Jude Fawley, returning home disillusioned and without his job. Advises him to try to become a 'licenciate'—partly qualified and humble curate—by study, taking care to avoid strong drink. *Jude the Obscure*

HILL, DICKY: Old neighbour of Maltster Smallbury at Norcombe, whose cottage and wooden cider house are pulled down. *Far from the Madding Crowd*

HILTON AND PIMMS: Telescope makers, supply Swithin St. Cleeve's telescope. *Two on a Tower*

HINTON, ADELAIDE: Childhood sweetheart and long-time fiancée of Edward Springrove, though both have outgrown the enthusiasm of their early love. About nine and twenty, she is pretty though paler and more self-possessed than her rival Cytherea Graye. Although jealous of her possession of Edward, she secretly marries rich Farmer Bollen, old enough to be her father, the day before Cytherea marries Manston. Some say she is unwilling to make do with a partner rejected by another. *Desperate Remedies*

HOLLOWTURNER, THE: A friend of Farmer Cawtree with whom he plays langerloo at Giles Winterborne's party, to the detriment of its refinement. *The Woodlanders*

HORSEYS: An ancient family which has decayed from nobility to obscurity. *Tess of the D'Urbervilles*

HUETT, IZZ: Pale, dark-haired dairymaid at Talbothays dairy, by nature the sauciest and most caustic of the four maids who are in love with Angel Clare. When Angel marries Tess Durbeyfield, Izz loses her gaiety, and when, estranged from Tess, he asks Izz to go to Brazil with him instead, she agrees, though her honesty in insisting that Tess loves him more than anyone makes him change his mind. Later she joins Tess and their friend Marian on Flintcome Ash farm, and with Marian later writes to warn Angel that Tess is being importuned by D'Urberville. *Tess of the D'Urbervilles*

HUMPHREY: A somewhat solemn young fellow, his legs sheathed in bulging leggings and carrying a hook and leather gloves, these being the marks of his furze-cutting trade. His comments first suggest to Eustacia Vye that Clym Yeobright would be a suitable match for her; and his remarks on his trade suggest to the near-blind Clym that he too should take to furze-cutting. *The Return of the Native*

HUNTWAY: A Cambridge friend of Ambrose Graye, now a clergyman living in Bloomsbury: Graye meets Cytherea Bradleigh while staying with him. *Desperate Remedies*

HURST, MRS.: Bathsheba Everdene's aunt at Norcombe, a smallholder. Bathsheba meets Gabriel Oak while visiting her. *Far from the Madding Crowd*

HURSTON, MRS.: Postmistress of Tolchurch, where Owen Graye and his sister go to live. *Desperate Remedies*

I

IVES, FARMER: His daughter hopes to attract the confirmed bachelor Farmer Boldwood, which costs her nights of tears and twenty pounds' worth of new clothes, but the money 'might just as well have been thrown out of the window'. *Far from the Madding Crowd*

J

JACKSON, MRS.: The lodging-house keeper at Budmouth where Owen and Cytherea Graye go to live. *Desperate Remedies*

JACOBS, CAPTAIN: The stout, red-faced captain of an excursion steamer who delays his boat's departure a little to wait for Cytherea Graye's brother Owen. *Desperate Remedies*

JAMES: A former admirer of Menlove whom she encourages very little once she finds he is married. *The Hand of Ethelberta*

One of Paula Power's menservants. *A Laodicean*

JAMES, COUSIN: Only surviving relative of Eunice Manston, he offers her a post as his housekeeper in America, which she is considering accepting at the time of her death. *Desperate Remedies*

JAMES, GRANDFATHER: Mrs. Ann Dewy's father, a stone-mason, whose clothes bear witness to his trade, being graduated in tints of stone colour and stiff with an accumulation of dust. Lives in a cottage by himself and is reputedly a miser. *Under the Greenwood Tree*

JANE: Adelaide Hinton's elderly servant. *Desperate Remedies*

A friendly maidservant at the Doncastles', who welcomes Picotee Chickerel to the servants' quarters as if she had known her five and twenty years. *The Hand of Ethelberta*

Humphrey's mother, who recollects hearing as a girl of the execution of Louis XVI. *The Return of the Native*

Parson Maybold's servant maid, rather local in manner, having been raised in the same village. *Under the Greenwood Tree*

JENKINS, SIMPKINS: A fellow 'improver' with Stephen Smith in an architect's office. *A Pair of Blue Eyes*

JENNY: A woman fieldworker of Marlott, too plain to risk seduction, unlike Tess Durbeyfield. *Tess of the D'Urbervilles*

JETHWAY, FELIX: A young farmer who loves Elfride Swancourt. She does not love him though perhaps she flirts with him, and considers him socially beneath her. He dies of consumption. *A Pair of Blue Eyes*

JETHWAY, MRS. GERTRUDE: A widow, well educated and of yeoman family. Dotes on her son Felix and blames the flirtatious Elfride Swancourt for his early death, attributing it to rejected love not consumption. Spending all her time travelling between the burial places of her family, she becomes mentally unbalanced, longs for revenge on Elfride, and happening to witness her uncompleted elopement trip with Stephen Smith, threatens to tell Elfride's second fiancé Henry Knight. Though accidentally killed by a falling tower, a letter posted before her death persuades Knight that Elfride has been compromised, and he jilts her. *A Pair of Blue Eyes*

JIM: A practising poacher, who works from the St. Peter's Finger public house. *The Mayor of Casterbridge*

JIM, COUSIN: Anne Garland, her mother and servant Molly are to take refuge at Cousin Jim's house inland when Bonaparte's invasion threatens the coast. *The Trumpet Major*

JIM, UNCLE: One of the masons at the Christminster stoneworks where Jude Fawley works. *Jude the Obscure*

JINKS, DAIRYMAN: An old gnarled character who wears a white fustian coat and yellow leggings, the only man of his circle who never dresses up in dark clothes for marketing. Observes somewhat satirically the return of George Somerset and his bride. *A Laodicean*

JOAKES, MRS.: An old acquaintance of Mrs. Smith; after snubbing her, becomes suddenly friendly on hearing of her son Stephen Smith's professional distinction. *A Pair of Blue Eyes*

JOE: A deposed keeper who frequents the St. Peter's Finger public house and talks over old times with ex-poachers. *The Mayor of Casterbridge*

JOE, UNCLE: One of the masons at the Christminster stone-works where Jude Fawley works. *Jude the Obscure*

JOHN: A fisherman of Knollsea. *The Hand of Ethelberta*

One of Lord Mountclere's keepers. *The Hand of Ethelberta*

A villager from Marygreen who knows Jude Fawley as a youth and meeting Jude later in Christminster is sad but not surprised that his scholastic ambitions have come to nothing. *Jude the Obscure*

Paula Power's manservant. He, Paula and Charlotte De Stancy are the only people who can work the castle tele-graph. *A Laodicean*

The driver of a road-waggon who gives the exiled Henchard news of his stepdaughter's coming marriage. *The Mayor of Casterbridge*

An Egdon Heath boy who acts in the Christmas mumming play, and 'needn't holler his inside out'. *The Return of the Native*

JOHN (H)OSTLER: The ostler at the Red Lion, Anglebury, a rickety person with a waistcoat of preternatural length, rather deaf. *The Hand of Ethelberta*

JOHNSON: A shipping agent, through whom Stephen Smith telegraphs to Elfride Swancourt. *A Pair of Blue Eyes*

JOHNSON, DAIRYMAN: His paddock faces Parkmaze Pool where John Woodward's brother is found drowned. *Under the Greenwood Tree*

JOHNSON, FARRIER-EXTRAORDINARY: A soldier in John Loveday's company. *The Trumpet Major*

JOHNSON, MATHILDA: A pretty woman, with brown or 'eel-coloured' eyes, black hair, a firm, sufficient nose and an attractive red mouth, though evidently older than her supposed twenty-two years. Gets engaged to Robert Loveday a fortnight after he comes ashore. Spending her coach fare on finery, she arrives at Loveday's home town in a cart, and is recognised by his brother John as a lady familiar in his regiment for her doubtful conduct; he insists that she leaves. Later jealousy of Robert and his new sweetheart Anne Garland make her point him out to a pressgang, though she then repents and helps Anne hide him. An actress by profession, she is glad to entangle and marry the credulous Festus Derriman. *The Trumpet Major*

JOLLARD, SQUIRE: His ale-cellar is cited by John Durbeyfield as being of comparable size to the D'Urberville family vault. *Tess of the D'Urbervilles*

JOLLY, BEAUBOY and FLIGHT, CAPTAINS: Members of John Loveday's regiment, with whom he has witnessed Mathilda Johnson behaving in a flighty manner. *The Trumpet Major*

JONES, COL. SIR MARTIN: Ancestor of the owner of Wyndway House; the bas-relief of his death at the moment of victory at Salamanca inspires philosophical meditations in the manservant. *The Hand of Ethelberta*

JONES, DR.: One of the doctors near Hintock who takes advantage of Dr. Fitzpiers's falling reputation in his adultery with Mrs. Charmond, by capturing patients up to his very door. *The Woodlanders*

JONES, MR.: A reflective man in spectacles who visits the Doncastles and discusses the butler Chickerel's character. *The Hand of Ethelberta*

JONES, NICK: His baby falls downstairs, and provides a subject of gossip for the De Stancys. *A Laodicean*

JONES, SADDLER-SERGEANT: A member of John Loveday's company. *The Trumpet Major*

JOPP, JOSHUA: Nearly engaged by Henchard as manager in his corn business, but is supplanted by Farfrae. Even when Henchard becomes Farfrae's enemy and competitor and employs Jopp after all, his resentment against both makes him a doubtful tool. His and Henchard's rashness brings ruin and they part on bad terms, but later Henchard lodges in Jopp's cottage, preferring his hatred to others' pity. Jopp reads Lucetta Farfrae's old love letters which Henchard has rashly trusted him to take to her, and his revelations about these directly lead to the scandal which ends in Lucetta's death. *The Mayor of Casterbridge*

JOSEPH: Coachman to the landlady of the Falcon inn, a lady with the demeanour of a duchess. *A Pair of Blue Eyes*

JOY, LADY JANE: Attends the Imperial Archaeological Association's meeting at Corvsgate Castle. *The Hand of Ethelberta*

JOYCE: Butler at Wyndway House where Ethelberta Petherwin visits and the Julians play for an impromptu dance. *The Hand of Ethelberta*

JOYCE, LAWYER: Town clerk of Casterbridge, a plain, frank man who persuades Farfrae not to set up a shop for Henchard who is his enemy. *The Mayor of Casterbridge*

JULIAN, CHRISTOPHER: Courts Ethelberta Petherwin before her marriage when she is a governess, but frequent quarrels and coolness part them. Still fascinated by her, however, and finding her a widow, he renews his courtship including the quarrels. He alone knows the secret of her humble birth and that the servants in her great house are really her brothers and sisters, but as her ambition is to provide for them all, his suit is hopeless, as his father has left him penniless and, being brought up to no profession, he supports himself and his sister Faith by teaching music, composing and playing the organ. Nevertheless he is disinterested in trying to save her from marriage with the dissipated old Lord Mountclere and to help her escape afterwards, but in vain. Ethelberta's sweet, simple young sister Picotee also loves him, though overshadowed by the dashing Ethelberta, and maintains correspondence with the Julians when they inherit a small income and go to live in Italy, so that when he returns two years later to become chief organist at Melchester Cathedral, he is cured of Ethelberta and decides to marry Picotee. A man whose appearance keeps in the rear of his mood—looking sad when he feels serene, and only serene when he really feels cheerful—he is romantic but not reckless, and accepts necessity philosophically. *The Hand of Ethelberta*

JULIAN, DR.: Father of Faith and Christopher, once a successful Sandbourne man, dies leaving his children unprovided for. *The Hand of Ethelberta*

JULIAN, FAITH: Christopher's sister, a small, neat, gentle girl who does not like to be seen wearing her spectacles. A musician herself, she is gifted with an unerring and powerful judgement of music. Destined to become an old maid, she rather disapproves of the dashing Ethelberta Petherwin whom her brother loves, but is happy to correspond with the simple, innocent Picotee Chickerel whom he eventually marries. *The Hand of Ethelberta*

K

KAIL, JONATHAN: An old dairyman at Talbothays dairy. *Tess of the D'Urbervilles*

KAYTE, GRAMMER: A neighbour of the Dewys, to whom Susan is sent to borrow some bigger candles. *Under the Greenwood Tree*

KEX, FARMER: Dick Dewy's wedding procession calls on him as a mark of respect. *Under the Greenwood Tree*

KEZIA: Dairyman Jinks's niece's daughter. *A Laodicean*

KIBBS, CAPTAIN JOB: A distant relative of Ann Avice Caro's father. Takes her for a trip to London on his lumpy craft. *The Well-Beloved*

KIBBS, MRS.: Wife of Captain Kibbs, accompanies her husband and Ann Avice Caro on a sea-trip to London. *The Well-Beloved*

KINGSMORE, ARTHUR: A singer who elopes with Lady Elfride Luxellian, Elfride Swancourt's grandmother, and dies soon after she does. *A Pair of Blue Eyes*

KITSON: A pig breeder, who attends Casterbridge market. *The Mayor of Casterbridge*

KNIBBS, BECK: A married dairywoman who works at Talbothays dairy but lives in her own cottage, a forthright damsel with woolly black hair and rolling eyes. *Tess of the D'Urbervilles*

KNIGHT, HENRY: A man of about thirty with dark brown hair and curly beard, his eyes and mouth seeming younger than his thoughtful brow. Qualified as a barrister, he also writes articles and reviews books but regrets not having excelled in any single field. As a youth he generously helps the boy Stephen Smith improve his basic education, continuing by correspondence while at Oxford, and later this patronage ripens into friendship. Meets Elfride Swancourt, as he is related to her stepmother, not knowing she is secretly engaged to Stephen. His intellectual superiority and more forcible character eclipse Stephen, she loves him and he reluctantly falls in love with her, especially when she saves him from a dangerous ledge on a high cliff. Hitherto a confirmed bachelor, he is insistent that he must be Elfride's first lover, is jealous at hints of an earlier engagement, and leaves her on learning of her elopement. After travelling to forget her, he meets Stephen, discovers his rôle in the story and that Elfride's innocence is intact, but as he and Stephen race to her home both are stunned to find she has married Lord Luxellian and died of a miscarriage. Though naturally a man of generosity and integrity, he appears cruel through allowing justice to supervene over his love, and resentment over his justice. *A Pair of Blue Eyes*

KNOCKHEELMAN, LIEUTENANT, CORNET FLITZENHART and CAPTAIN KLASPENKISSEN: Foreign members of the York Huzzars who dazzle village maidens with their gallantry and stories of their fatherland. *The Trumpet Major*

KNOWLES: One of the three first-class London draughtsmen whom Somerset employs to assist him regardless of expense in preparing his competition plans for restoring De Stancy Castle. Has a beard. *A Laodicean*

L

LADYWELL: A young painter of good family who falls in love with Ethelberta Petherwin, is proud of being in the secret of her poetic authorship, paints her portrait, and likes to be teased about her. After many vicissitudes—a mistaken belief in his rival Neigh's success, optimism at being promised her answer in a month, gloom at overhearing her promise the same to old Lord Mountclere—he tries to forget her, but at her private wedding is accidentally present, 'looking as sick and sorry as a lily with a slug in its stalk'. *The Hand of Ethelberta*

LARK, TABITHA: Daughter of a Welland dairyman, who

as a pretty half-grown girl is employed to read aloud to Lady Constantine, her speech being remarkably sharp and fluent. Because of her musical talent she is the church organist, and later is trained in London as a musician, becoming one of 'the phalanx of Wonderful Women who had resolved to eclipse masculine genius altogether and humiliate the brutal sex to the dust'. As she also becomes a beautiful young woman, no doubt Swithin St. Cleeve will marry her after the death of Lady Constantine. *Two on a Tower*

LAURA: A little blue-eyed girl of eight or so who is the first embodiment of the child Jocelyn Pierston's ideal of beauty. *The Well-Beloved*

LAWSON, SAM: Sells Reuben Dewy a second-hand cask for cider that proves to be much more rotten than expected. A man for a drop of drink, 'good but not religious good'. Now dead. *Under the Greenwood Tree*

LEAF, JIM: One of Mrs. Leaf's babies, who dies 'rather youthful' aged four hours twenty minutes, but whose memory and birthdays are faithfully kept by Mrs. Leaf and Thomas. *Under the Greenwood Tree*

LEAF, MRS.: A melancholy widow who can be seen every morning 'her eyes mooning out through the panes of glass like a pot-sick winder-flower'. She has had twelve children, all except Thomas dying very young 'either before they were born or just after'. *Under the Greenwood Tree*

LEAF, THOMAS: Only surviving son of Mrs. Leaf, a weak, lath-like form consisting chiefly of a human skeleton and a smock frock. A well-meaning young man, he sings treble better than any boy or woman, is known for having 'no head' and keeping his smocks amazingly clean. *Under the Greenwood Tree*

LEAT, MRS. ELIZABETH: Postmistress at Carriford, a female who sports several unique diseases and afflictions, makes traditional use of her position in noting everyone's mail, nor can customers escape her (as Manston tries to do) by posting letters at Budmouth, for her son, a post-office clerk there, reports back to her. *Desperate Remedies*

LEDLOW, FARMER: His house is visited first by the carol-singing choir. *Under the Greenwood Tree*

LEDLOW, MRS.: The farmer's wife, counts her money and reckons her week's marketing expenses during the first lesson in church. *Under the Greenwood Tree*

LEDLOW, OLD DAME: May be the farmer's wife in *Under the Greenwood Tree*. An aunt of Farmer Shinar, lives at Mellstock where Mother Cuxom attends her party. Is called Toad-skin because of her yellow, freckled face. *The Mayor of Casterbridge*

LESTER: Stone and marble mason, sells Sergeant Troy an expensive tombstone for Fanny Robin. *Far from the Madding Crowd*

LE SUEUR, LUCETTA: *see* Templeman, Lucetta

LEVERRE: A widower of Jersey, with one son, Henri. He marries Marcia Bencombe. Younger than she, he likes her to appear as young and fresh as possible. Dies leaving her a very small income. *The Well-Beloved*

LEVERRE, HENRI: Stepson of Marcia Leverre, *née* Bencombe, who when widowed brings him up alone on a small income, in Jersey and Paris. He becomes a French teacher at Sandbourne and falls in love with Avice Pierston—French lessons are the pretext for their meetings. Ill and poor, Henri is not acceptable to her family, and when Avice obeys her mother in agreeing to marry Jocelyn Pierston, Henri comes to bid her farewell. Unwisely over-exerting himself, he has to take refuge in her cottage, and they decide to elope. *The Well-Beloved*

LEVERRE, MRS.: *see* Bencombe, Marcia

LEWELL, BILL: Works at Talbothays dairy. *Tess of the D'Urbervilles*

LICKPAN, JOSEPH: Second son of Robert Lickpan the pig-killer, will never be able to use the 'Family Joke' which depends on the pig-killer's name being Bob. *A Pair of Blue Eyes*

LICKPAN, LEVI: Uncle of the pig-killer, whose cleverness is shown in devising an unopenable snuff box. Tallest man ever seen in the district, he sleeps on the floor with his feet poking out on the landing until the day of his death. *A Pair of Blue Eyes*

LICKPAN, ROBERT: Carrier and pig-killer, of an old family of pig-killers. Brings Stephen Smith to Endelstow Rectory. Also has a son, Bob. *A Pair of Blue Eyes*

Grandfather of the pig-killer, a pig-killer himself in days when pig killings were pig killings, and invents the 'Family Joke' on the subject. *A Pair of Blue Eyes*

Father of the pig-killer, a pig-killer himself for more than five and forty years. *A Pair of Blue Eyes*

'LITTLE FATHER TIME': *see* 'Time, Little Father'

LIZZY: Dances with Richard Dewy at the Dewys' Christmas party. *Under the Greenwood Tree*

LOCKHAM: A yeoman volunteer, fellow-trooper with Festus Derriman who teases him with stories of the invading French during the false invasion alarm. *The Trumpet Major*

LONG, LAWYER: Pennyways tries but fails to consult him on behalf of Troy and his position as a man presumed drowned. *Far from the Madding Crowd*

A Casterbridge councillor. *The Mayor of Casterbridge*

LONGWAY, SOLOMON: An old man of sixty-nine, who works for Henchard. *The Mayor of Casterbridge*

LOVEDAY, JOHN: At thirty-two he is the elder son of Miller Loveday, a trumpet-major in the army. Falls in love with Anne Garland while his regiment is stationed near his old home, but his thoughtful, responsible character does not attract her, and she considers him rather beneath her socially. When his brother Bob returns from sea and revives Anne's childhood love for him in spite of social considerations and his engagement to another, John spoils his own chances (with Anne) and furthers Bob's by recognising his fiancée as a woman of bad reputation and sending her away. However Bob, remorseful at John's unhappiness and inspired by patriotism to volunteer for service on Nelson's flagship against the French, renounces his favour with Anne to his brother. Ironically John is just for the first time beginning to prevail with Anne (aided by reports of Bob's infidelity elsewhere) when Bob changes his mind and reclaims her, John nobly standing aside yet again. His sterling qualities are eclipsed by his fickle, cheerful brother, though it is hardly surprising that his constant renunciations fail to win a very human girl like Anne. Goes with his regiment 'to blow his trumpet till silenced for ever upon one of the bloody battlefields of Spain'. *The Trumpet Major*

LOVEDAY, MR. ('MILLER'): Owner of Overcombe Mill, father of John and Robert. A hale, fifteen-stone widower of fifty-five or sixty, with a face capable of immense changes of expression. He lets part of his mill house to Widow Garland, is an attentive neighbour and eventually marries her. *The Trumpet Major*

LOVEDAY, ROBERT (BOB): Miller Loveday's younger son, a sailor on a merchant vessel. Though tenderly remembered by Anne Garland his childhood sweetheart, he finds and becomes engaged to Miss Mathilda Johnson within his first two weeks on land, on his way home, but learning that her morals are suspect he turns with practised rapidity to Anne, succeeding here where his sober brother John has failed. However a narrow escape from the pressgang awakens his patriotic feelings, and learning of John's feelings he joins the navy to sail against Bonaparte, giving up Anne to John. News of his engagement to a baker's daughter disgusts Anne, who is just reconciling herself to the grateful John

68

when Bob changes his mind again, returns to supplant his noble and retiring brother, and is eventually forgiven. An ingenuous young man, he is generous when the necessity can be impressed upon him, and has the natural gaiety that takes all sorrows lightly. *The Trumpet Major*

LUCY: The Julians' cousin, estranged from them for many years, but she leaves them three hundred pounds a year in her will. On this they go to live in Italy. *The Hand of Ethelberta*

LUCY, JANE, FLORA, EVANGELINE: Girls who successively seem to embody Jocelyn Pierston's ideal of beauty. *The Well-Beloved*

LUXELLIAN, THE HONOURABLE KATE and MARY: Katie and Polly, the two little daughters of Lord Luxellian who particularly love Elfride Swancourt: for their sake he first considers marrying her. *A Pair of Blue Eyes*

LUXELLIAN, HUGO: An ancient Luxellian of Edward the Second's reign. *A Pair of Blue Eyes*

LUXELLIAN, LADY: First wife of Lord Luxellian, a squire's daughter. Limp, thin and with 'skim-milky eyes and complexion', she is really sickly and dies at the age of thirty-one. *A Pair of Blue Eyes*

LUXELLIAN, LADY ELFRIDE: A daughter of a former Baron Luxellian; elopes with Kingsmore, a singer, and dies giving birth to Elfride Swancourt's mother. *A Pair of Blue Eyes*

LUXELLIAN, LORD GEORGE: A 'strappen fine gentleman' of towering build, a bitter enemy of little Simeon the mason, whom he curses 'as familiarly and neighbourly as if he'd been a common chap'. Weighs five hundredweight, coffin and all, when he comes to be buried. *A Pair of Blue Eyes*

LUXELLIAN, LORD SPENSER HUGO: Fifteenth Baron

Luxellian. In appearance resembling a good-natured commercial traveller of the superior class, his attraction is his musical laugh. Manly, open and sincere at least, he admires Elfride Swancourt, a distant relation. Dotingly fond of his daughters, he is rather indifferent to his wife and after her death courts Elfride, at first rather for the sake of his children who love her, but after their marriage his love for her grows and he is heartbroken at her sudden death. *A Pair of Blue Eyes*

M

MACFARLANE, SANDY; LEITH, ARCHIBALD; DUNBLEEZE, WILLIE; and MACFREEZE, MAITLAND: Scottish acquaintances of Farfrae's, mentioned as disproving Scottish luck as all were drowned, murdered or otherwise unlucky. *The Mayor of Casterbridge*

MAIL, MICHAEL: A bowed and bent member of the Mellstock choir in which he plays second violin. *Under the Greenwood Tree*

MANSTON, AENEAS: Illegitimate son of the rich Miss Aldclyffe, left by her pseudonymously with a widowed schoolmistress. She follows his career with interest but makes no contact with him until the death of her father releases her from obligations to her family, and she manages to install him as her steward. An extremely handsome man of about thirty, with a wonderfully clear complexion, he has a reputation as a libertine and is secretly married to Eunice, a third-rate actress, but he honourably controls his passionate love for Miss Aldclyffe's companion Cytherea Graye. His wife eventually protests at their separation, using her assumptions about his parentage, which she reveals later to him, to enlist Miss Aldclyffe in her interests. Partly by mistake, partly by carelessness, he misses meeting her train, so that she has to go to an inn, and believing she is dead in the fire that just then destroys the inn, he rejoices in his freedom until she reappears, having escaped, and in his disappointment he strikes and kills her. Thereafter he uses all methods, fair and foul, to win the reluctant Cytherea Graye who at last marries him, only to have the news that Eunice has not died in the fire discovered on their wedding night. Far from ensuring she is assumed dead, however, Manston suddenly has to deceive an unexpected if doubtful witness of his murder by producing a woman to impersonate Eunice, saving his neck but losing Cytherea. Made desperate by threatened discovery of this impersonation, he prepares to escape but is seen disposing of Eunice's body, and after a long pursuit in which he tries to abduct Cytherea, he is captured, writes a full confession and commits suicide in prison. *Desperate Remedies*

MANSTON, MRS.: The widow of a schoolmaster, on whose doorstep Miss Aldclyffe leaves her illegitimate baby Aeneas. Later meets Miss Aldclyffe, whom she knows as Jane Taylor, several times to report on the child's progress. *Desperate Remedies*

MANSTON, EUNICE: Wife of Aeneas Manston, originally from Philadelphia, a third-rate actress, of whom he tires soon after their marriage—she lives apart under the alias Mrs. Rondley. Besides her fading beauty, she possesses a nagging tongue and a weakness for brandy, so that Manston, honourably repressing his love for Cytherea Graye, is unenthusiastic about being reunited with her. However, she effects reunion by pressure on his employer Miss Aldclyffe whom she guesses to be his mother. Offended that he is absent when she arrives, Eunice goes to a nearby inn but leaves it before it burns down. Less lucky in meeting her husband immediately afterwards, she is murdered by him. At first believed dead in the fire, she has in fact been seen by two people after that, and the woman produced by Manston later is an impersonator brought in to confuse the witness of her murder. *Desperate Remedies*

MARIAN: A plump, jolly milkmaid, eldest of those at Talbothays dairy, in love with Angel Clare. Disappointed in his ignoring her and marrying Tess Durbeyfield, she takes to drink, is dismissed from the dairy and has to take to the roughest kind of farm work. Loyal though coarse, on hearing of Tess's separation from Angel, she encourages her to seek work with her at Flintcombe Ash farm. Later she and another former dairymaid friend write anonymously to warn Angel of Tess's persecution by her would-be lover D'Urberville. *Tess of the D'Urbervilles*

MARTHA: The nurse who tends Susan Henchard in her last illness. *The Mayor of Casterbridge*

MARTIN, FARMER GILES: A limberish man who used to go rather bad upon his legs, and whose daughter gets married above her station to Parson St. Cleeve. *Two on a Tower*

MARTIN, MR.: A customer of the Mellstock butcher Mr. Haylock. *Under the Greenwood Tree*

MARTIN, MRS. ('GAMMER'): Maternal grandmother of Swithin St. Cleeve, looks after him and is still an active woman at eighty years old. *Two on a Tower*

MATT: A lad appealing for work at Talbothays dairy, approved by Angel Clare for having no established family, not so much as a surname. *Tess of the D'Urbervilles*

MAYBOLD, MR. ARTHUR: Vicar of Mellstock, a good-looking young man with courageous eyes, timid mouth and neutral nose. Much more zealous and active than the previous incumbent, and one of his reforms is to replace the instrumental musicians of the choir by an organ, to the choir's disappointment. His love for the schoolmistress Fancy Day grows when he sees her established as the new organist, but being out of touch with village gossip he proposes marriage only after her secret engagement to Dick Dewy. Though she agrees, tempted by his social position, he learns immediately afterwards of her engagement and unselfishly suggests she reconsider, just as she confesses and changes consent to refusal. He cannot however bring himself to marry Fancy to Dick. *Under the Greenwood Tree*

MAYBOLD, MRS.: Mr. Maybold's mother, lives near Budmouth Regis and takes up a fancy for keeping bees (pleasantly disguised as an economical wish to produce her own honey). *Under the Greenwood Tree*

MELBURY, THE FIRST MRS.: Mother of Grace Melbury. Formerly a sweetheart of Giles Winterborne's father, won from him unfairly by George Melbury. A 'child of a woman' who would 'cry like rain if so be he huffed her'. *The Woodlanders*

MELBURY, GEORGE: A rich timber-merchant, thin with slightly stooping figure and a small nervous mouth, he characteristically moves in sudden jerks. Having won his first wife unfairly from Giles Winterborne's father, he intends in compensation that his only daughter Grace shall marry Giles. However he repents this intention seeing that Grace's expensive education has refined her above the level of an awkward yeoman like Giles, especially when Giles loses the lease of some cottages which have increased his income. He promotes Grace's marriage to Doctor Fitzpiers, whom he embarrasses by his rusticity, but is bitterly angry on hearing of Fitzpiers's adultery with the landowner Mrs. Charmond. Resolving against polite custom to fight his daughter's battles, he appeals to Mrs. Charmond, then quarrels with and strikes Fitzpiers, who then goes abroad. Hoping naïvely for a divorce for Grace under a new law, he encourages her to be reconciled with Giles, only to cause the more disappointment when divorce proves impossible. All his efforts are in vain, for eventually Grace and Fitzpiers are secretly reconciled and go to live in a distant part of England. *The Woodlanders*

MELBURY, GRACE: Daughter of George Melbury, beautiful or not beautiful according to her health and spirits, of a fair, clear complexion with a small, delicate mouth showing too little assertiveness for her own good. Luckier than her acquaintance Marty South, her innate qualities are cultivated by education, until she finds her native village and home rustic and uncongenial, but is not unwilling to marry her childhood sweetheart Giles Winterborne, in spite of his awkwardness. However her father changes his mind about this match, declares she is now too refined for a yeoman, and encourages her to marry Dr. Edred Fitzpiers, although her feeling for him is rather fascination than love, and her loyalty to Giles persists. After marrying Fitzpiers she finds he has become the lover of the landowner Mrs. Charmond, but is more disgusted than jealous, feeling once more attracted to Giles and the unsophisticated rustic way of life. Led by her father to hope for a divorce, Grace encourages Giles's courtship, but finding divorce impossible, she cannot face her penitent husband's return, and runs away. She remains in hiding in Giles's hut while he, chivalrously camping outside, becomes ill and dies. Blaming her excessive prudery for keeping him from shelter, Grace tells her husband that she has been Giles's mistress, and later when he guesses the truth, is still reluctant to see him. However they are reconciled eventually and Marty South is left to mourn Giles alone. Grace is a gentle girl who combines modern nerves with primitive feelings, a contradiction aggravated by her artificial education, so that she concludes she would have been happier working like Marty South in the woodland. *The Woodlanders*

MELBURY, MRS. LUCY: A placid woman who has been the motherless Grace Melbury's much-loved nurse, so that George Melbury persuades her to marry him for his daughter's benefit. This 'arrangement' works well, and he is often influenced by her quiet advice. *The Woodlanders*

MENLOVE, LOUISA: A quick-eyed, light-haired, slightly built lady's-maid, very skilful at her work and even more adept at entangling young men and deceiving her employers. At first works for Lady Petherwin, also tending Ethelberta Petherwin; later works in the same house as Chickerel the butler, bedazzles his young son Joey and learns that they are Ethelberta's father and brother. Her fiancé Tipman, Lord Mountclere's valet, earns money for their wedding first by revealing this relationship to his master, then by concealing it, when Mountclere decides to marry Ethelberta anyway. But Menlove breaks this secrecy after a quarrel with Chickerel which does not prevent but makes difficult Ethelberta's new rôle as viscountess. *The Hand of Ethelberta*

MICHAEL: The old milkman of Anglebury. *The Hand of Ethelberta*

MILD, LIEUTENANT: A young lieutenant of artillery, a diffident, inexperienced, rather plain-looking fellow, who therefore causes no embarrassment when acting opposite Paula Power in *Love's Labour's Lost*—however, probably by secret arrangement, the ardent Captain De Stancy steps into his rôle at the last moment. *A Laodicean*

MILLER, SOBERNESS and TEMPERANCE: Women working on Bathsheba Everdene's farm, characterised by Henery Fray as 'Yielding women—as scarlet a pair as ever was'. *Far from the Madding Crowd*

MILLS: Servant of Mr. Torkingham, Vicar of Welland. *Two on a Tower*

MINCING, PARSON: Marries Bathsheba Everdene and Francis Troy in Bath. *Far from the Madding Crowd*

MITCHELL, JOB: A neighbour of Miller Loveday. *The Trumpet Major*

MOCKRIDGE, NANCE: Works for Henchard wimbling hay bonds. She has rather a bad character, and mischievous disposition—she is a moving spirit in the 'skimmington-ride' pageant that leads to Lucetta Templeman's death. *The Mayor of Casterbridge*

MOLLY: Servant to Miller Loveday after he marries Widow Garland. Accompanies her mistress and Anne Garland in the evacuation of the coast during the invasion scare. *The Trumpet Major*

MONEY, MARY ANN: Bathsheba Everdene's charwoman. To think of her was to get good-humoured; to speak of her was to raise the image of a dried Normandy pippin. Has a constant joke about looking for a husband. *Far from the Madding Crowd*

MOON, MATTHEW: Works on Bathsheba Everdene's farm. He is a singular framework of clothes with nothing of consequence inside them, who speaks 'as the rustle of wind among dead leaves'. *Far from the Madding Crowd*

MORE, JIMMY: A blacksmith, used to employ the father of a large family who economises on expensive church funerals by becoming a Nonconformist. *A Laodicean*

MORRIS, MRS.: Housekeeper to Miss Aldclyffe. An elderly woman of lengthy smiles and general pleasantness, kindly and rather fussy. *Desperate Remedies*

MORRS'S: A public house where Enoch drinks. *Under the Greenwood Tree*

MOULIN, M.: A well-formed, reflective man with a grey beard, once a handsome French courier; marries Mrs. Chickerel's sister Charlotte and keeps an hotel in Rouen. *The Hand of Ethelberta*

MOULIN, MME. CHARLOTTE: She and her French husband keep the Hotel Bold Soldier in Rouen. Her face is an English outline filled in with French shades. She welcomes her nieces Ethelberta Petherwin and Cornelia Chickerel for a visit, rather preferring the less fashionable simple country girl Cornelia to her sister. *The Hand of Ethelberta*

MOUNTCLERE, THE HON. EDGAR: A man in his fifties, with iron-grey hair and practised social manner, Lord Mountclere's younger brother, attends the Imperial Archaeological Association's meeting at Corvsgate Castle, then fearing to be cut out of the succession by his brother's impending secret marriage to Ethelberta Petherwin, he brings her brother Sol Chickerel with him so they can dissuade the couple from marrying, but this inharmonious journey—for he is as proud as Sol is republican—is too late. *The Hand of Ethelberta*

MOUNTCLERE, LORD: A viscount of at least sixty-five, of dapper, sly appearance and vicious reputation. He pursues Ethelberta Petherwin, and learns, through his valet and her former lady's-maid, of her humble origins. Piqued by the rivalry of others, however, his dishonourable intentions are turned into a wish to marry her, which he manages speedily and privately. Cunning enough to forestall her impulsive escape from him on learning on their wedding night of his dissipation, he is not as strong-willed as she, and is eventually tamed, reformed, and made prosperous by her management. *The Hand of Ethelberta*

MYNTERNE, CONJURER: A celebrated conjurer with power over obstinate butter churns, consulted by Dairyman Crick's grandfather, and now dead. *Tess of the D'Urbervilles*

N

NAN: Fancy Day's charwoman. *Under the Greenwood Tree*

NAPPER, MRS.: A middle-aged acquaintance of Neigh's, who knows everyone. *The Hand of Ethelberta*

NAT: A labourer who accidentally brings down his hammer on John Smith's hand while they are driving a pile. *A Pair of Blue Eyes*

NEIGH, ALFRED: A handsome, grim-natured, cynical and phlegmatic man of the world, who at thirty-five is attracted against his will by Ethelberta Petherwin. She is repelled on a secret inspection of his country 'estate' to find it a tract hired out for kennelling and knackering, and learning that his family has made its fortune in tanning and that he particularly dislikes lower-class women, she concludes that he will be disgusted by discovering her own humble origins. By his fascination, however, he wrings at least an ambiguous answer from her, only to retire frustrated on finding the same answer given to two other suitors. Even on hearing of her humble birth he is concerned enough to press money on her father to help him prevent her marriage to the vicious Mountclere. *The Hand of Ethelberta*

NELLY: A Casterbridge girl whose love affair is saved by Farfrae who kindly employs her sweetheart and his old father in the town instead of their prospective employment at a great distance. *The Mayor of Casterbridge*

NEWSON, ELIZABETH JANE: Daughter of Susan Henchard and Richard Newson, not knowing that she is illegitimate because her father 'bought' her mother from her real husband Henchard. To conceal all this from her, after Newson's reported death, Susan seeks out Henchard again and they 'remarry'. After her mother's death Elizabeth Jane is told by Henchard that she is his own daughter, which he then believes, but learning his mistake he turns against her, venting irritation against her unpolished behaviour. Unhappy because of this and also because of her un-prosperous love for her stepfather's enemy Farfrae, she sets herself to self-improvement, first by books, then by going as companion to Lucetta Templeman. Farfrae falls in love with the livelier Lucetta, and Elizabeth Jane bears this with dignity, her disapproval of their marriage later stemming from knowledge of Lucetta's early commitment to Henchard. After this, living alone, she eventually wins the affection of Henchard, now a broken, ruined man deserted by all but her, so that, hoping to keep her for himself, he tells her returned father Newson that she is dead. Her discovery of this deception rouses her inflexible moral convictions against him and she will not forgive the double deception. After Lucetta's death, she and Farfrae are again drawn together by their similarly sober, prudent natures, and they marry. Her implacability towards Henchard at her wedding is finally discouraging to him and he is dead when, in some remorse, she seeks him out in his countryside exile. Though harsh in this, she is equally severe with herself, enduring philosophically the 'unhappy substitutions' fate brings her, so that 'what she had desired had not been granted her, and that what had been granted her she had not desired'. Taking her final fortune calmly, she passes on to others the lesson of making limited opportunities endurable. *The Mayor of Casterbridge*

NEWSON, RICHARD: A light-hearted, open-faced sailor, who hears Michael Henchard offering to sell his wife Susan and, believing she will be happier with him, 'buys' her for five guineas. After many years in Canada they return to England where, as their relationship is troubled by Susan's learning of its illegality, he decides to go to sea again, and allows a report of his death to stand uncorrected. Returning years later a rich man he enquires after Susan and their daughter Elizabeth Jane. Henchard has persuaded Elizabeth Jane that he is her father, and tells Newson that she is dead. Because of his trusting disposition Newson accepts this unsupported statement, leaves, and only learns the truth months later. He returns in time for Elizabeth Jane's marriage to Farfrae and lends the celebration a gaiety that is of his making rather than theirs. Eventually he settles in a port to be near the sea. *The Mayor of Casterbridge*

NINEMAN, CORPORAL: It is at his funeral at Casterbridge that Mr. Penny first hears the 'Dead March'. *Under the Greenwood Tree*

NOAKES, JACOB: A fellow-yeoman-trooper of Festus Derriman, in domestic life farmer of Nether-Moynton. *The Trumpet Major*

NOBBS: Lady Constantine's coachman. *Two on a Tower*

NOCKETT AND PERCH: Builders and contractors for whom Sol Chickerel works. *The Hand of Ethelberta*

NUNSUCH, JOHNNY: A sad little boy in pinafores whom Eustacia Vye keeps reluctantly tending her signal bonfire as a pretext for keeping it. He witnesses without understanding Wildeve's visit to Eustacia after her marriage and her refusal therefore to open her door to her exhausted mother-in-law Mrs. Yeobright. He reports Mrs. Yeobright's embittered dying words to her son. His mother blames Eustacia's witchcraft for his persistent ill-health. *The Return of the Native*

NUNSUCH, SUSAN: A widespread woman whose stays creak like shoes whenever she stoops or turns, and as she wears pattens summer and winter to preserve her boots, she is a woman of noisy construction to dance with at the bonfire party. Blaming Eustacia Vye as a witch for her son Johnny's ill-health, she sticks a stocking-needle deep into her arm in church to break the spell. When this does not work she melts an effigy of Eustacia, who just at that time drowns herself. *The Return of the Native*

NYTTLETON, MR.: One of Miss Aldclyffe's solicitors, experienced and habitually bland: the 'culpable slyness' of his boyhood is 'moulded by Time, the Improver, into honourable circumspection'. *Desperate Remedies*

O

OAK, GABRIEL: Grandfather of Gabriel Oak, the shepherd; is remembered as 'just such a nice unparticular man' as his grandson. *Far from the Madding Crowd*

Father of Gabriel Oak the shepherd, himself a shepherd tending the flocks of large proprietors till his death. *Far from the Madding Crowd*

A man of twenty-eight, of rather large build who curtails

his dimensions by his modest, unassuming bearing, and whose moral colour is a kind of pepper and salt mixture. While starting his own sheep farm he proposes marriage to a poor neighbour's niece, Bathsheba Everdene, but she does not love him. Both leave the district and alter their fortunes: Gabriel loses his flock and money through the viciousness of an untrained sheepdog, and travelling to seek work he saves some burning ricks which belong to Bathsheba, who has inherited a large farm and employs him as her shepherd. His character matures in adversity from its initial neutrality to a social self-sufficiency; he continues constant to Bathsheba in spite of her new superiority, her imperiousness and her preference for two more eligible suitors. As the one she marries, Sergeant Troy, is dashing but ignorant of farming, it is left to Gabriel once more to save the farm harvest from devastating storm, helped only by Bathsheba, while Troy and the farm hands ignore his warnings and lie in drunken sleep. Regaining confidence after his misfortunes, he hangs back from seizing opportunities because of his ties to Bathsheba, though after Troy is reported dead Bathsheba in her depression makes him her bailiff, as does her neighbour and suitor Farmer Boldwood. After Boldwood, maddened by disappointment, kills the returning Sergeant Troy, Gabriel, who is less shaken because more independent, carries independence to an extreme pitch of generosity by planning to emigrate to avoid gossip. Bathsheba however induces him to propose marriage again. From seeming the soberest and most insignificant of Bathsheba's three suitors, Gabriel survives and succeeds because of his moderation and self-reliance. Their marriage is based on the substantial affection arising from first knowing the rougher sides of each other's character, and not the best till later on. *Far from the Madding Crowd*

O'FANAGAN, MRS. TARA: A tactless lady with a gold-clamped tooth, who forms part of the rather heterogeneous party gathered by Lord Mountclere to meet Ethelberta Petherwin at his country house. *The Hand of Ethelberta*

OLIVER, GRAMMER: Mr. Melbury's servant, who has two facial aspects, one of a soft and flexible kind for indoors, the other with stiff lines and corners, for the men outside. Her unusually large skull tempts Dr. Fitzpiers to buy the right to 'anatomise' it after her death, but during an illness she panics and sends Grace Melbury to 'buy' her skull back, thus bringing Grace and Fitzpiers together. *The Woodlanders*

ONMEY, MERCY: Fancy Day's bridesmaid. *Under the Greenwood Tree*

ORCHARD, JANE: Her 'little maid' takes Thomasin Yeobright's letter of rejection to Diggory Venn. *The Return of the Native*

ORCHARD, WILLY: A little boy who spreads the story of seeing a 'red ghost'—probably in fact the reddleman Diggory Venn. *The Return of the Native*

OUNCE, CAPTAIN: Master of the steamer *Spruce* that runs from Sandbourne to Knollsea. A comparative stranger to the treacherous Knollsea Bay, he tries to land there during a storm, especially as he is bringing a doctor for his wife, but turns back because of the danger and the news that he is the father of a newborn baby boy: thus his passengers Sol Chickerel and Edgar Mountclere are frustrated in trying to take this short cut to Knollsea to prevent Ethelberta Petherwin's marriage to Lord Mountclere. *The Hand of Ethelberta*

P

PADDOCK, JEREMIAH: A villager of Welland, who reports seeing Sir Blount Constantine locking his wife out of the house in a fit of anger. *Two on a Tower*

PARIDELLES: An old family that used to own land near King's Hintock and is now decayed. Retty Priddle the dairymaid is a descendant of the Paridelles, as Tess Durbeyfield is of the D'Urbervilles. *Tess of the D'Urbervilles*

PENNY, MRS.: Wife of the cobbler. *Under the Greenwood Tree*

PENNY, ROBERT: A bespectacled member of the Mellstock choir, short and stout and much irritated by his wife's frequent references to his small size. A shoemaker by trade, he claims to recognise anyone simply by their foot or boot. *Under the Greenwood Tree*

PENNYWAYS, BAILIFF: Dismissed for stealing barley by Bathsheba Everdene soon after she acquires her farm—this gives her the opportunity to act as her own bailiff. Because he is untrustworthy Bathsheba will not listen to his news that her husband Sergeant Troy is not dead as believed but alive; thus his chance of preventing confusion and tragedy is frustrated, and Troy soon afterwards bribes him to silence. *Far from the Madding Crowd*

PERCOMB, MR.: A barber of Sherton Abbas whose finical clothes mark him out of place in the country. 'Perruquier to the aristocracy', his clientele among the local gentry is not in fact enough to fill his children's mouths so he has a second little shop behind his house for cutting labourers' hair at twopence a time. Successfully persuades Marty South to sell him her long rare-coloured hair to be resold to Mrs. Charmond. *The Woodlanders*

PERKINS, JANE: Hopes to attract the confirmed bachelor Farmer Boldwood and works at him for two months like a slave, to no avail. *Far from the Madding Crowd*

PETHERWIN, LADY: At first furious at her son's elopement with her governess Ethelberta Chickerel, but relents when he dies almost immediately, her own husband also dying soon afterwards. Takes the girl widow under her wing, sending her abroad to acquire polish, then keeps her as her companion, on condition she never mentions her humble relatives, most of whom are servants. Discovering Ethelberta has published a volume of poems, now celebrated, she is shocked and destroys a will in her favour, so that although on her deathbed she writes to her brother and legatee asking him to allow Ethelberta a large sum (which he does not), she leaves her only the lease of her town house. *The Hand of Ethelberta*

PETHERWIN, MRS. ETHELBERTA: One of the ten children of the poor Chickerel family, her father being a butler. She is unusually clever, becomes a pupil-teacher, then as governess in a great family elopes with her employer's young son, but he dies on their honeymoon. Her widowed mother-in-law, relenting at this catastrophe, takes Ethelberta to live with her on condition of never mentioning her lowly family, after further polishing her education and manners on the Continent. Boredom leads both to Ethelberta's renewed interest in an old suitor Christopher Julian and to her publishing a volume of very clever and rapidly celebrated poems. Lady Petherwin is angry at discovering this so that, though they are reconciled, she dies leaving Ethelberta the lease of her town house but no money. Ethelberta provides for herself and family by giving public performances as a lady romance-narrator, and saves for her young sisters' education by taking in lodgers, still keeping this secret to preserve her aristocratic persona by employing only her own brothers and sisters as servants. The lease running out, she considers which of her suitors, the painter Ladywell or man-of-the-world Neigh, she can marry, but decides on the old and dissipated Viscount Mountclere who still wants to marry her though knowing of her humble origins. Their marriage is so private that her relatives and friends, appalled at his shocking reputation, arrive too late to prevent it. Ethelberta on learning more of her husband tries to escape to a safe bargaining position abroad but is foiled by his superior cunning, and has to stay and fight for her position. Some years later she has dominated him, regulated his way of life, overhauled and economised his estate, and reigns as 'my lord and my lady both' by sheer iron will-power. Something of an adventuress, she eventually comes through her sufferings to a useful and active position—she is also writing an epic poem in her spare time—because of her roots in the country and the affectionate, united Chickerel family. *The Hand of Ethelberta*

PETHERWIN, SIR RALPH: A city gentleman, who dies unforgiving towards his son who has eloped with the governess Ethelberta Chickerel and predeceased him, leaves his money unconditionally to his wife. *The Hand of Ethelberta*

PETHERWIN, YOUNG: Young son of Lady Petherwin who elopes with the governess Ethelberta Chickerel and dies on their honeymoon. *The Hand of Ethelberta*

PHILEMON, TIMOTHY TITUS: Bishop of Bristol, as noted on Bob Garland's unused marriage licence. *The Trumpet Major*

PHILLOTSON, MR. RICHARD: Jude Fawley's first schoolmaster, who goes to Christminster hoping to enter a college and implants the same fatal ambition in Jude too. Ironically Jude later persuades his beloved cousin Sue Brideshead to become Phillotson's teaching assistant in order to keep her in his neighbourhood, and Phillotson, though much older than her, falls in love with her and persuades her to marry him. By this time a much-chastened and disappointed man with a thin, careworn face, he is physically repulsive to the over-fastidious Sue, and he generously allows her to leave him for Jude, divorcing her, although his 'immoral' lack of vindictive objection costs him his job and reputation. The clergyman of Jude's old village charitably gives him employment at a penurious salary, and later his reconsideration of social pressures as well as his persisting attraction to Sue make him accept her penitential return and remarriage to him, though aware of her continued repulsion. *Jude the Obscure*

PHILLOTSON, MRS. SUE: *see* Brideshead, Sue

PIERRE: A French valet and temporary lover of the lady's-maid Menlove, challenged to a duel by his rival, a courier. Menlove never finds out which one kills the other. *The Hand of Ethelberta*

PIERSTON, AVICE: Avice the third, daughter of Ann Avice, and granddaughter of the original Avice Caro. Unites her grandmother's cultivation, sensibility and delicacy with her mother's charm and mystery, so that Jocelyn Pierston, now growing old, is led against his better judgement to agree to her mother's proposal of an arranged marriage between them. Avice also agrees, from duty and prudential reasons, but is appalled to learn his real age; a former attachment to Henri Leverre is revived, and on the eve of her marriage she elopes with him just as Jocelyn forty years earlier has abandoned her grandmother. The shock of this kills her mother, and Avice continues shaken in nerves by remorse all her life. *The Well-Beloved*

PIERSTON, ISAAC: Marries Ann Avice Caro secretly, then they quarrel and separate, but later Ann Avice admits the marriage to her suitor Jocelyn Pierston (no relation). The birth of their child and Jocelyn's generous endowment of a stone-cutting business reconciles them, though Isaac continues an irascible husband until success in business makes him indifferent to domestic circumstances. Dies in an accident in his own quarry, leaving his family quite rich. *The Well-Beloved*

PIERSTON, JOCELYN: One of a family native to the Portland peninsula, the family business being quarrying its famous rock. Jocelyn's artistic gift develops from carving this rock, and after a good education, partly abroad, he eventually becomes a famous sculptor. The bane of his life however is that his artistic vision of female beauty is linked with peculiar fickleness, for this ideal beauty never settles in one woman for long. His engagement as a young man to an educated but unspoilt Portland girl Avice Caro is therefore broken by his detection of ideal beauty in the chance-met Marcia Bencombe, and they elope together, but before marrying they quarrel, the impression of beauty disappears, and she returns home. After twenty years of pursuit and disappointment Jocelyn falls under the spell of the late Avice Caro's daughter Ann Avice, who is less cultured but more flirtatious, less ingenuous and more seductive than her mother. Ironically she is as fickle as he, but soon tires of him whereas his fancy remains for once fixed upon her. Though a poor, unsophisticated laundress, she is also less frank than her mother and conceals her secret marriage to a stone-mason Isaac Pierston when agreeing to become Jocelyn's housekeeper in London. Discovering this, he returns her to her husband in Portland, where her child by Isaac is born soon afterwards, Jocelyn financing a stone-cutting business to cement their reconciliation. Now rich and famous, Jocelyn returns after another twenty years to be bewitched yet again by the widowed Ann Avice's daughter Avice the third. On the eve of at last fulfilling his broken engagement to her grandmother and his rejected courtship of her mother by marrying the unenthusiastic Avice, Jocelyn is thwarted by her elopement with Henri Leverre, stepson of his old sweetheart Marcia Bencombe. Ann Avice, who has favoured his marriage, is killed by the shock, and after the funeral Jocelyn meets Marcia again, who nurses him through an illness which destroys not only his youthful appearance but his sense of beauty and susceptibility to the ideal. They marry in their old age for convenience, and Jocelyn spends an undisturbed, comfortable retirement in demolishing the inconvenient ancient beauties of his native place. *The Well-Beloved*

PIERSTON, MR.: Jocelyn Pierston's father, a stone merchant who makes his gifted son an allowance until his sculptures can make an income, but is otherwise rather a hard taskmaster, if trustworthy, just but ungenerous. Known as something of a miser, he leaves Jocelyn an unexpectedly large fortune on his death. *The Well-Beloved*

PIERSTON, MRS.: *see* Caro, Ann Avice

PINE-AVON, MRS. NICHOLA: Granddaughter of Lord Hengistbury, widowed soon after her marriage, an intellectual, emancipated but gentle and thoughtful woman, with fine eyes and chestnut hair. Attracted by Jocelyn Pierston, who also begins to find his elusive ideal beauty in her, because of a misunderstanding she suddenly discourages him, discovering her mistake only too late when he has become obsessed with Ann Avice Caro. Is not too falsely proud to apologise, but in vain, though Jocelyn's friend Somers sees and admires her, and Jocelyn advises him to marry her, as 'a woman of individuality and earnest instincts' who is ready to turn from the world of fashion to the world of art. Alas, marriage to Somers and motherhood eclipse her emancipated individuality making her vicariously conventional again on behalf of their row of young daughters. *The Well-Beloved*

PITNEY, MRS.: Angel Clare's godmother, wife of the Squire, a vain, kind woman who, prophesying a distinguished career for him, leaves him jewels in trust for his wife. *Tess of the D'Urbervilles*

PLAMBY, LADY: A woman with theories, who pets her servants far too much, lending them books and sending them to picture exhibitions which, according to her friends, 'only makes them dissatisfied'. *The Hand of Ethelberta*

POORGRASS, JOSEPH: Works on Bathsheba Everdene's farm. A desperately bashful man, who blushes deeply when faced with any woman. Given to moralising, especially when drunk, he likes to think himself a man in the Bible. Sent to fetch Fanny Robin's coffin from Casterbridge workhouse for burial, he stops so long for a drink that he misses the funeral. *Far from the Madding Crowd*

POPP, CAPTAIN: An officer of the 501st, marries one of Jocelyn Pierston's ideals of beauty, Elsie Targe, and takes her to India. *The Well-Beloved*

POWER, ABNER: Brother of Paula Power's father, less business-like but a brilliant engineer. Dogged and self-willed, he lives in a poor area of Geneva where he is discreetly silent about his neighbours, a group of anarchist assassins. Appreciating this, they employ him to make the explosive device used in a notorious assassination. Later becoming conservative and respectable, he leaves the fraternity but while destroying his explosives is burnt and scarred beyond recognition—in many ways an advantage. Thereafter successful in the guano trade in Peru, he later visits his very rich orphaned niece Paula Power and encourages her to marry Captain De Stancy for his old name and prospective title, trying to discourage her architect suitor George Somerset. However, discovering De Stancy has an illegitimate son and prospective blackmailer William Dare, he tries by threats to send Dare abroad, but finding Dare knows of his anarchist past, abruptly throws up his projects and returns to Peru. *A Laodicean*

POWER, JOHN: Member of Parliament, industrialist and railway engineer, a strict Baptist who uses some of his immense fortune to encourage Nonconformism in his area. Wishes his only daughter Paula to be baptised by total immersion but after his death she cannot bring herself to it. *A Laodicean*

POWER, PAULA: A beautiful young woman with abundant brown hair, a modern type of girl who though strong-willed is torn between different points of view, being, like the church at Laodicea, neither hot nor cold in her commitments. Thus she declines from admiration of her father's technological achievements and Baptist faith after his death, being unable to undergo baptism by total immersion, but neither does she become totally immersed in the romantic mediaeval atmosphere of her home, De Stancy Castle, though it attracts her. Attracted also by the young architect

George Somerset, she employs him to restore her castle, but will not commit herself to marrying him, partly because of the rival courtship of Captain De Stancy, descendant of the castle's original owners. Tricked into believing Somerset has demanded money from her, she agrees to marry De Stancy, but learns just before the wedding that Somerset's misdeeds are all fabrications of the youth Dare, and demanding that Dare be arrested discovers he is De Stancy's illegitimate son. She breaks off their marriage. Remorseful and disregarding convention, she pursues the bewildered Somerset across Europe, explains all and suggests they marry. Staying at an inn on their return home, they see the castle burn down, and decide to build a completely modern mansion instead: thus Paula will live according to the modern, compromising philosophy of 'imaginative reason' —though characteristically her proclamation even of this compromise concludes with regret for lost mediaevalism. *A Laodicean*

PRIDDLE, RETTY: Youngest of the living-in dairymaids at Talbothays dairy, auburn-haired and delicate. In love with Angel Clare, when he marries Tess Durbeyfield she tries to drown herself, and though saved in time seems to go into a decline. *Tess of the D'Urbervilles*

R

RACHEL: The nurse-girl of about thirteen who helps Thomasin Wildeve with her baby. Borrows her mistress's gloves for a maypole dance and loses one, so that Thomasin's suitor Venn is able to find it. *The Return of the Native*

RANDALL, DAN: Keeper of Sherton turnpike, the sleepiest man between there and London, and a guaranteed delay to any night traveller. *Far from the Madding Crowd*

RANDLE, ANDREW: A stammering man, comes to work on Bathsheba Everdene's farm, having been turned away from his last place for asserting plainly that his soul was his own and other iniquities. *Far from the Madding Crowd*

RAUNHAM, MR. JOHN: Rector of Carriford, a relation of Miss Aldclyffe on the poorer, paternal side; there is a polite indifference between them. A solitary bachelor but gallant and courteous, he is attracted by Cytherea Graye's beauty, a feeling he will not admit even in the privacy of his own thoughts. Jointly with Springrove summons detectives to find the truth about Manston's first wife. Unwillingly accepts the legacy of Miss Aldclyffe's estate, only to turn it over for the administration and use of Springrove and Cytherea when they marry. *Desperate Remedies*

RAVENSBURY, JOHN: A schoolfellow of George Somerset, and cousin of the De Stancys, whom Charlotte De Stancy was to have married. Intends to be a parson, but, always very unfortunate, he dies suddenly. *A Laodicean*

RICHARD: A drinker at the St. Peter's Finger public house. *The Mayor of Casterbridge*

ROBIN, FANNY: A very pretty, gentle, yellow-haired girl, servant at Weatherbury farm, although only a few days after Bathsheba Everdene's arrival she runs away to follow her lover Sergeant Troy. She almost keeps him to his promise to marry her but, one of life's born victims, spoils her own opportunity by waiting at the wrong church. She next appears, very ill and pregnant, creeping painfully to Casterbridge workhouse where she dies. Troy, now married to Bathsheba, finds his wife has brought Fanny's coffin to their farm to await burial and guessed his paternity of Fanny's stillborn child. He declares himself morally more Fanny's husband than Bathsheba's, but the flowers he plants on her grave, strangely washed away by a storm, are replanted by Bathsheba in tribute to her rival who has triumphed at least in death. *Far from the Madding Crowd*

ROLLIVER, MRS.: Keeps a public house with only an off-licence, so that she always has to pretend those drinking illegally indoors are her personal guests. *Tess of the D'Urbervilles*

RONDLEY, MRS.: *see* Manston, Mrs. Eunice

ROOBERT: Miss Aldclyffe's coachman, a melancholy man in cheerful livery, who prefers drowning his sorrows to living them down. *Desperate Remedies*

ROOTLE: The Budmouth dentist, who has abstracted some 'worn-out nether millstones' from Mrs. Garland's jaw. *The Trumpet Major*

RUNT, CHRISTOPHER: An onlooker and well-wisher at Edward Springrove's marriage to Cytherea Graye. *Desperate Remedies*

RYME, JOSEPH: A friend of Mr. Penny, he takes the treble violin part in Chalk-Newton church choir for two and forty years. *Under the Greenwood Tree*

S

ST. CLEEVE, DR. JOCELYN: Paternal great-uncle of Swithin St. Cleeve, the doctor is a narrow, sarcastic and shrewd bachelor who has amassed a comfortable fortune by long and extensive medical practice in a manufacturing town. His disgust with the low birth of Swithin's mother is altered by reports of Swithin's scientific talent, but hearing also of the attachment of Lady Constantine, and being a misogynist himself, he bequeaths an income to Swithin conditional on his remaining unmarried until he is twenty-five. Dies just after an unsuccessful voyage for his health to the Cape, where he recommends Swithin to go and study. *Two on a Tower*

ST. CLEEVE, THE REV.: Curate to the late Vicar of Welland, he offends the local gentry by marrying a farmer's daughter, and taking offence in his turn, throws up his profession, takes to farming, and drops down dead in a thunderstorm—said to be divine retribution for his defection. Also his wife, daughter of Farmer Giles Martin, who 'socked and sighed and went out like a snoff'. *Two on a Tower*

ST. CLEEVE, SWITHIN: Son of Parson St. Cleeve and Farmer Martin's daughter, orphaned and cared for by his old grandmother. A very beautiful youth of twenty who is also very clever and absorbed in studying astronomy, in which he hopes in spite of poverty to make his name. Lady Constantine, who owns the tower he uses as an observatory, falls in love with him but he thinks only of astronomy until she is widowed, when pointed local gossip prompts him to return her love, though she is nearly ten years his senior. Practical as well as visionary, he insists that marriage will be less of a distraction than a love affair, but agrees to keep the marriage secret until he can distinguish himself and support his wife. Receiving news of a legacy conditional on his remaining single, he refuses it, and keeps his secret against suspicion and hostility from Lady Constantine's brother Louis, and would-be suitor Bishop Helmsdale. When she discovers that a mistake in the date of her widowhood makes their marriage invalid, and that the legacy is open to Swithin, and renounces him, he is still determined to remarry her at all costs. However, she remains adamant until Swithin departs to study in a South African observatory promising to marry her five years later, when ironically she discovers she is pregnant. Swithin loses all hope of regaining her when she writes of her plight and necessary hasty marriage to Bishop Helmsdale. Returning a successful astronomer to find her widowed again but noticeably aged after three years, he resolves to marry her after all, which comes as a shock that overstrains her heart and kills her. His early declaration that astronomy and

Lady Constantine are his two allegiances remains true; his gentleness and romantic sensibility are matched with scientific capability; his respect for the bleak immensities of space makes him stoically endure the merely human delays and discomforts of their intrigue so much better than Lady Constantine. Probably he will marry young and intelligent Tabitha Lark. *Two on a Tower*

SAM: A turf or peat-cutter, he uses the special heart-shaped spade, though he helps with furze-work too. *The Return of the Native*

SAMWAY, SAM: One of Farmer Boldwood's men, he tries to break the news to his master of Troy's return, and succeeds in preventing him shooting himself. *Far from the Madding Crowd*

SARAH: She and Anny are the girlhood friends of Arabella Donn, who advise her to entrap Jude Fawley into marriage by becoming pregnant. *Jude the Obscure*

SAUNDERS, EZEKIEL: Formerly a clockmaker of Caster-bridge; one of his clocks owned by the Day family is familiarly called after its maker. *Under the Greenwood Tree*

SCRIBBEN, SAMMY: One of Ann Avice Caro's admirers, who will help her with the heaviest laundry work if she lets him, but, not knowing his own strength, he twists a tablecloth in two while wringing it. *The Well-Beloved*

SCRIBBEN, WILLIAM: A Portland islander, called in vain by Avice Pierston when she is trapped by a rock crevice. *The Well-Beloved*

SEABORN: A native of the Portland peninsula who hopes to see Jocelyn Pierston marry Avice Caro—in vain. *The Well-Beloved*

SEAMORE, GRANNY: An old woman with wrinkled cheeks and brass-rimmed spectacles through which she observes Derriman's pursuit of Anne Garland. *The Trumpet Major*

SEAWAY, ANNE: A handsome, well-built, dark woman in her thirties, something of an adventuress though just deprived of her respectable housekeeping job by the death of her employer when Manston, her old acquaintance, approaches her. Not knowing he has murdered his first wife Eunice, she is puzzled but agrees to impersonate her. Suspicious at his panic when others notice she is darker than Eunice, she spies on him, seeing him bury Eunice's body and attack a detective. Instead of escaping, her innate generosity makes her help the injured detective, and though arrested on suspicion, she is later exculpated by Manston's confession. *Desperate Remedies*

SEEDLING, AMBY: An occasional helper at Talbothays dairy. Is in love for two years with Izz Huett whom he follows to Flintcombe Ash, but she ignores him, being hopelessly in love with Angel Clare. *Tess of the D'Urbervilles*

SEVERN, EARL OF: Sergeant Francis Troy may be his illegitimate son. *Far from the Madding Crowd*

SHINAR, FARMER: Attends the market in Casterbridge—may be the same as Farmer Shiner. *The Mayor of Casterbridge*

SHINER, FARMER FRED: Aged about thirty-five, farmer and churchwarden, a character chiefly composed of a crimson stare, vigorous breath and a watch chain. Is far from religious when drunk, as witness his discourtesy to the carol-singing choir on Christmas Eve, but shows zeal in urging the vicar to substitute a church organ for instrumental musicians—his ulterior motive being his love for Fancy Day, the prospective organist. *Under the Greenwood Tree*

SILCHESTER, BISHOP OF: He is wrongly supposed to be related to the mysterious Ethelberta Petherwin. *The Hand of Ethelberta*

SIMEON: A shrivelled old mason who works for John Smith. *A Pair of Blue Eyes*

SMALL, MR.: A profound writer who never prints his books. Attends the Imperial Archaeological Association's meeting at Corvsgate Castle. *The Hand of Ethelberta*

SMALLBURY, ANDREW: Probably Jacob Smallbury's brother; said to have known Gabriel Oak as a boy. *Far from the Madding Crowd*

SMALLBURY, BILLY (WILLIAM): The oldest of the Smallbury family, a maltster in winter and a farm labourer in summer, still active in spite of his great age (around ninety). He has 'frosty white hair and beard over his gnarled figure like the grey moss and lichen upon a leafless apple tree', and all neighbours have to forget their difference to join in soothing him when offended. *Far from the Madding Crowd*

Grandson of the old maltster, son of Jacob; a child of forty or thereabouts who remembers Gabriel Oak's family at Norcombe. Possesses a cheerful soul in a gloomy body. *Far from the Madding Crowd*

SMALLBURY, JACOB: Son of the old maltster, a young man of about sixty-five with a semi-bald head and one tooth on the left side of his jaw. Used to be sworn brothers with Gabriel Oak's father. *Far from the Madding Crowd*

SMALLBURY, JOE: Is said to have known Gabriel Oak's father even better than Jacob Smallbury. *Far from the Madding Crowd*

SMALLBURY, LYDDY (LYDIA): Great-granddaughter of the old maltster and youngest daughter of the younger Billy Smallbury. Servant–companion to Bathsheba Everdene. Less classically beautiful than her mistress, she has the lovely complexion of the typical English country girl, and though more elastic in nature than Bathsheba she is less liable to go to extremes. Her giddiness encourages Bathsheba to send the fatal Valentine to Farmer Boldwood, but she is a great comfort to Bathsheba in her miseries over Sergeant Troy. *Far from the Madding Crowd* smart: A shoemaker, who frequents the Three Mariners at Casterbridge. *The Mayor of Casterbridge*

smith, general sir stephen fitzmaurice: A Caxbury gentleman: Stephen Smith is named after him only because his grandfather was the General's gardener, so Parson Swancourt's assumption that Stephen must be related to the General causes later disappointment. *A Pair of Blue Eyes*

smith, john: A skilled workman, a stone-mason of Parson Swancourt's parish. Neither as stereotyped in character nor as narrow in his calling as a townsman, he can turn his hand to brick-laying, tree-felling and gardening. Brown as autumn as to skin, white as winter as to clothes, his stalwart healthiness is a sight to see. When his son Stephen, who has had a good education and works in a London architect's office, falls in love with Parson Swancourt's daughter, John's humble status is a major obstacle to the match. Later he moves to a nearby town where he gains some celebrity through Stephen's later achievements abroad. *A Pair of Blue Eyes*

smith, mrs.: Addressed by Parson Swancourt as Jane and by her husband John as Maria. Comes of a family of well-to-do yeomen, though left an orphan. She worked in a dairy as a girl, and as a mason's wife is careful to 'keep herself up'. Still comely in middle age, she seems possessed of sound common sense, but inclined to be argumentative against unflattering views: thus she considers Stephen her son is the equal and later the superior of the parson's daughter. *A Pair of Blue Eyes*

smiths, the leaseworthy: A noble family to which Parson Swancourt is wrongly convinced Stephen Smith must belong. *A Pair of Blue Eyes*

smith, stephen fitzmaurice: A London architect's poor young assistant who, staying in Parson Swancourt's Wessex house while surveying his church, falls in love with the parson's daughter Elfride. As a boy he has attended a national school but his education is improved to gentlemanly standards by the personal and epistolary guidance of his older friend Henry Knight, thus Swancourt never imagines he is the son of a humble mason of his parish. When this is revealed Swancourt forbids Stephen's courtship of Elfride, and they set out to elope, but on the journey she has second thoughts and turns back. After this secret attempt he takes a post in India to achieve prosperity as quickly as possible, but revisits England to find Elfride engaged to his friend Knight. His final return, honoured and distinguished for architectural successes, is unhappy until he finds that distorted rumours of the early elopement have made Knight jilt Elfride. Feeling that 'life without Elfride would never be any great pleasure to himself, or honour to his Maker', he hurries down to Wessex, only to find Elfride has married Lord Luxellian and died of a miscarriage. Because of his lowly origins and patchy education Stephen's love is admiring and submissive, 'rather after a feminine than a male model', and he is eclipsed by the dominating Knight, though the more faithful. *A Pair of Blue Eyes*

SNEAP, LUKE: A choir player, he breaks his new fiddle bow on the wedding psalm when Parson Wilton brings home his bride. *Two on a Tower*

SNEWSON, MRS.: Mrs. Charlotte Swancourt's maid. *A Pair of Blue Eyes*

SNIFF, VASHTI: Fancy Day's bridesmaid, a young lady who blushes cream-colour, and wears yellow bonnet ribbons. *Under the Greenwood Tree*

SNOOKS: A neighbour of Miller Loveday. *The Trumpet Major*

SOMERS, ALFRED: Jocelyn Pierston's friend and confidant, a painter and eventually an academician though rather popular than distinguished. A long-leased bachelor, he abruptly decides to marry Nichola Pine-Avon whom

98

Jocelyn is regretfully unable to love, and becomes a middle-aged family man with spectacles and a row of daughters tailing off to infancy. At the same time he abandons his personal and peculiar style and executes pleasing middlebrow landscapes that earn him a lot of money. *The Well-Beloved*

SOMERSET, GEORGE (SENIOR): A famous painter, who in spite of his dependence on colour in his art chooses to live in the fogs and gloom of London. *A Laodicean*

SOMERSET, GEORGE: A nice young man of good features and eloquent brown eyes, with the singular thoughtfulness in spite of his youth typical of introspective modern man. After being tempted by various branches of art, he settles belatedly to architecture. Meets and falls in love with the beautiful and rich Paula Power who wishes him to restore her inheritance, the mediaeval De Stancy Castle, though she agrees that he shall compete for the commission with Havill, her late father's architect. Somerset's rival in love is Captain De Stancy, descendant of the castle's former owners, and De Stancy's unscrupulous illegitimate son Dare plans to remove Somerset, whose assistant he temporarily becomes, by betraying his designs to and ensuring the victory of his competitor Havill. However the two architects' designs are judged equal, but Havill, stung by remorse, gives up the half of the commission he is awarded. Somerset's opportunities of courtship are thwarted when Paula goes travelling away from the castle, and Dare's next plot is more successful, forging Somerset's name to a demand for money and retouching his photograph libellously. Paula's friend Charlotte De Stancy accidentally discovers the truth and though loving Somerset herself heroically restores him to Paula's favour just in time to prevent her marriage with De Stancy, inculpated with the guilty Dare. Still ignorant of these machinations and Paula's beliefs, Somerset is pursued by her across Europe until she catches him, apologises, and they marry. Like Paula, Somerset is a passive figure in the plots and counterplots, and like her takes a selective interest in ancient and modern, romantic and practical. *A Laodicean*

SOMERSET, JOHN: George Somerset Junior's great uncle, who being interested in genealogy gives a written pedigree to his brothers and sisters. *A Laodicean*

SOUTH, JOHN: Marty's father. The last of a line of nominees in whose lifetime Giles Winterborne's family hold leases and income from certain cottages, these being forfeit on John South's death. In old age and illness he is obsessed by a tree overshadowing his window, but when Giles and Dr. Fitzpiers cut the tree down, the shock kills him. *The Woodlanders*

SOUTH, MARTY: Nineteen-year-old daughter of old John South, whose face has the characteristic fullness of expression developed by a life of solitude, though her hands, features and character, all originally delicate, are marked by her manual work in the woodlands, not moulded by education as in her rich friend Grace Melbury. Not strictly beautiful, she has unusually lovely hair of exactly the same shade as the rich landowner Mrs. Charmond. To her Marty sells her own hair to make a false hairpiece, motivated by despair of ever attracting Giles Winterborne, who loves her refined friend Grace. Stoically silent, she sees Giles pine and eventually die of illness and exposure, all her rival's fault. Marty's silent loyalty outlasts Grace's sorrow and remorse—and indeed Marty's revelation of the false hair sale disrupts Grace's husband's affair with Mrs. Charmond and reconciles him to Grace, who quickly forgets Giles. Marty like Giles is part of the woodland life from which Grace grows away; 'Marty South of all the women in Hintock and the world, had approximated to Winterborne's level of intelligent intercourse with Nature. In that respect she had formed his true complement in the other sex.' *The Woodlanders*

SPEEDWELL, LADY IRIS: The brightest hostess in London, an old friend and confidante of Jocelyn Pierston. At her dinner party his reconciliation with Mrs. Pine-Avon is prevented by news of Avice Caro's death. *The Well-Beloved*

SPINKS, ELIAS: Member of the Mellstock choir who walks perpendicularly and dramatically, and is considered to be a scholar, having once kept a night school. Is given to irony and sarcasm. *Under the Greenwood Tree*

SPRINGROVE, EDWARD: Son of Farmer Springrove, is given a good education, furthered by his gift for drawing, and becomes an architect. Dark, handsome and rather untidy, he is clever but lacks the ambition and enthusiasm to be really successful. He befriends a young colleague Owen Graye and falls in love with his sister Cytherea, but cannot commit himself because of a long-standing engagement to his childhood sweetheart Adelaide Hinton. The rich Miss Aldclyffe, who wishes Cytherea to marry her steward (really her illegitimate son) Manston, makes Springrove's marriage to Adelaide a condition of assistance to his ruined father. Adelaide secretly marries a rich farmer but too late for Springrove to win back Cytherea, who marries Manston, but on their wedding night Springrove brings news that Manston's first wife has not, as supposed, died in a fire. He later discovers the apparently reconciled first wife is an impostor, and is at last on hand to save Cytherea when Manston, hunted for the murder of his real first wife, tries to abduct her. He is rewarded by marrying her. Miss Aldclyffe's bequest of her estate, refused by Cytherea, is made over for the couple's use and administration by the next legatee Mr. Raunham, so Springrove's lack of architectural ambition is no hindrance to their prosperity. *Desperate Remedies*

SPRINGROVE, FARMER EDWARD: Father of Springrove the architect, formerly landlord of an inn that has decayed with the ending of coaching, now a farmer and cidermaker. A poet with a rough skin, gentle and kindly by nature, though sturdy and tough by circumstance. His thatched inn burns down accidentally so that the steward

Manston's wife, then staying there, is believed burnt too, as are the adjacent cottages which are not insured and which he is obligated by his lease to rebuild. Miss Aldclyffe uses this obligation as a threat, secretly offering to waive it if his son will marry his fiancée Adelaide Hinton as planned, and renounce Cytherea Graye. The shock of the fire and threat of ruin works on Farmer Springrove's nervously thoughtful nature, undermining his confidence, but he recovers his usual pensive equability when his son agrees to the bargain and removes the threat. *Desperate Remedies*

SPRINGROVE, MRS.: Wife of Farmer Springrove, used to serve in their later disused inn. Expects Clerk Crickett to succumb to his often-widowed new wife, but herself predeceases him. *Desperate Remedies*

STAFF, COL.: A colonel who teases Ladywell about his acquaintance with the poetess 'E'—actually Ethelberta Petherwin. *The Hand of Ethelberta*

STAGG, JACK: A fellow stone-mason with Jude Fawley. *Jude the Obscure*

STAINER, ANDREW: Has a pig that goes 'as clean out of his mind as the cleverest Christian could go'. *A Pair of Blue Eyes*

STANNER, SERGEANT: Parades as a recruiting officer in Budmouth, and sings a satirical comic song at Miller Loveday's party, 'but in spite of his satire, he fell at the bloody battle of Albuera a few years after this pleasantly spent summer'. *The Trumpet Major*

STANNIDGE: Taciturn landlord of the Three Mariners in Casterbridge. *The Mayor of Casterbridge*

STANNIDGE, MRS.: Landlady of the Three Mariners, an easy woman to strangers, she remains 'fixed in her armchair as if she had been melted into it when in a liquid state and could not now be unstuck'. *The Mayor of Casterbridge*

STARKS, JIM: An Egdon Heath boy, acts the Valiant Soldier in the Christmas mumming play, who in his ardour for genuine histrionic art comes down on the stone floor with force enough to dislocate his shoulder. *The Return of the Native*

STEPHEN: A carpenter employed in De Stancy Castle in mediaeval times. *A Laodicean*

STOCKWOOL, GRAMMER: Lives with Ann Avice Caro in her cottage, and looks after it while she is away. *The Well-Beloved*

STOCKWOOL, RUTH: A nurse, born on Portland, and neighbour of Ann Avice Pierston (*née* Caro) whom she tends during her last illness. *The Well-Beloved*

STOKE, SIMON: Alec D'Urberville's father, who makes a fortune and chooses the name D'Urberville at random to attach to his own plebeian name, which eventually it supplants, Stoke-D'Urbervilles becoming simply D'Urbervilles. Thus his family are not related to the genuine old D'Urbervilles nor to their descendants the Durbeyfields. *Tess of the D'Urbervilles*

STOKE-D'URBERVILLE: *see* D'Urberville

STONEY, JOHN: A Portland islander, called in vain by Avice Pierston when she is trapped in a rock crevice. *The Well-Beloved*

STRAW, DAVID: Stable boy at the Red Lion, Anglebury. *The Hand of Ethelberta*

STRICKLAND, CAPTAIN: Leader of the Casterbridge company, ninety strong, mustered against Bonaparte's invading army. *The Trumpet Major*

STRONG, CAPTAIN: The captain of Lord Mountclere's yacht, the *Fawn*. *The Hand of Ethelberta*

STRONGWAY: One of Lord Mountclere's keepers. *The Hand of Ethelberta*

STROODEN, TIM: Foreman of works on Miss Aldclyffe's

estate, demoted to less responsible foremanship when Manston comes as steward. An onlooker at the wedding of Springrove and Cytherea Graye. *Desperate Remedies*

STUBB: Farmer of Duddle Hole and a yeoman volunteer, fellow-trooper of Festus Derriman who teases him with stories of the invading French during the false invasion alarm. *The Trumpet Major*

STUBBERD, CONSTABLE: A Casterbridge constable, a shrivelled old man. *The Mayor of Casterbridge*

SUSAN: The neighbour's pink daughter who helps in Mrs. Garland's house in the mornings. *The Trumpet Major*

SWANCOURT, CHRISTOPHER: Rector of East and West Endelstow, father of Elfride. Hearty, hasty, and for a widower of fifty, handsome, his complexion being 'the usual neutral salmon-colour of a man who feeds well—not to say too well—and does not think hard'. An admirer of ancient lineage, he has eloped with Elfride's noble mother, but now values social approval and material advantage so that, discovering his young architect visitor Stephen Smith is the son of a humble local parishioner, he forbids his courtship of Elfride. He remains ignorant of their unsuccessful attempt at secret marriage because he is busy making a successful secret marriage himself with the homely but very rich Mrs. Troyton. His new wife's cousin Henry Knight supplants Stephen in Elfride's affections. After Knight's later misunderstanding and horror of Elfride's earlier elopement, Mr. Swancourt has to bring her home from a vain attempt to pursue and plead with Knight, and shocked at her behaviour he is always afterwards a stern father, until she marries Lord Luxellian. Is last seen at Elfride's funeral, looking much older than his years. *A Pair of Blue Eyes*

SWANCOURT, ELFRIDE: Daughter of the Rector of Endelstow, pretty with light brown hair and very blue eyes, she has a mobile sympathetic nature that carries her to extremes of feeling, but not for long. Though blamed by his mother for the death of consumption of Felix Jethway, whom she has rejected, Elfride first falls in love with the young architect Stephen Smith, a match opposed by her family because of his humble origins. They attempt secret marriage but her courage fails on the way so they return undetected except by Mrs. Jethway, her enemy. Her intense sorrow when Stephen leaves for India to improve his income for her sake is distracted by her father's remarriage to a rich widow and their new social life. She has written a novel and finds that her stepmother's cousin Henry Knight is Stephen's admired friend and hostile reviewer of her novel. Piqued and interested, she comes to love him instead of the less impressive Stephen. She saves his life on a dangerous cliff, but when he learns through Mrs. Jethway of her former elopement, he leaves her. In desperate simplicity she pursues him but is taken home by her angry father, and lives at home in disgrace until the widowed Lord Luxellian marries her. She dies of a miscarriage soon afterwards. A creature of extremes, she loves Stephen too hastily, and transfers her affections too soon, is too open in her affections and too secretive about past mistakes, yet her resilience often saves her. *A Pair of Blue Eyes*

SWANCOURT, GEOFFREY: One of Parson Swancourt's ancestors who loses a barony for his family by an unfortunate joke. *A Pair of Blue Eyes*

SWANCOURT, MRS. CHARLOTTE: Formerly the widowed Mrs. Troyton, who owns all that part of Endelstow that is not Lord Luxellian's. Marries Parson Swancourt, though a few years older than he is. A very dark, portly, comfortable-looking woman, she has a good-humoured face and a whimsical sense of humour. Promotes Elfride Swancourt's match with her relation Henry Knight, but after his strange jilting of Elfride and her desperate pursuit of him, she becomes cool to her. A woman of the world as to knowledge and the opposite as to action. *A Pair of Blue Eyes*

SWEET, LAWYER: A thriving young lawyer, quite the dandy, who is publicly attentive to humble Mrs. Smith after her son Stephen becomes distinguished. *A Pair of Blue Eyes*

SWEETAPPLE, DAIRYMAN: Jack Griggs drops Joan Dummett in his cow barton while carrying her home from a party. *The Mayor of Casterbridge*

T

TALL, LABAN: Usually known as 'Susan Tall's husband', having no individuality worth mentioning. Fond of music, but very much under his wife's thumb. *Far from the Madding Crowd*

TALL, SUSAN: She calls herself five and twenty, looks thirty, passes as thirty-five and is forty. A critical gossip who never shows conjugal tenderness in public, perhaps because she has none to show. *Far from the Madding Crowd*

TALLER, BET: Has a dress made just like one of Fancy Day's (though of miserably cheap stuff) so that Fancy cannot wear hers on that account. *Under the Greenwood Tree*

TANGS, OLD TIMOTHY: Top sawyer working for Mr. Melbury. *The Woodlanders*

TANGS, YOUNG TIMOTHY: Bottom sawyer and son of old Timothy; engaged to Suke Damson. When he guesses on their wedding day that she has been Dr. Fitzpiers's mistress he is jealous, and later, mistakenly believing Fitzpiers still to be meeting Suke, he sets a man-trap which almost catches Fitzpiers's wife Grace. Emigrates with Suke to New Zealand. *The Woodlanders*

TARGE, COLONEL: A middle-aged gentleman, father of Elsie. *The Well-Beloved*

TARGE, ELSIE: A brown-haired young woman of nineteen, who embodies the schoolboy Jocelyn Pierston's ideal of beauty. She marries Captain Popp and goes to India. *The Well-Beloved*

TAYLING: One of Miss Aldclyffe's solicitors, younger than his partner Nyttleton. *Desperate Remedies*

TAYLOR: A servant in Lord Mountclere's household. *The Hand of Ethelberta*

TAYLOR, DR.: A dean who attends the Imperial Archaeological Association's meeting at Corvsgate Castle. *The Hand of Ethelberta*

TAYLOR, JANE: *see* Aldclyffe, Miss Cytherea

TAYLOR, MR.: His effects are being sold by auction when Michael Mail nods a greeting to the auctioneer and is put down as having bought Mr. Taylor's feather bed, bolster and pillows. *Under the Greenwood Tree*

A doctor on the fringes of whose practice Dr. Fitzpiers sets up his own practice. *The Woodlanders*

TAYLOR, TINKER: A decayed church ironmonger, who seems to have taken a blasphemous turn from his original religious state. Drinks with Jude Fawley when he is drowning his sorrows after abandoning his scholastic ambitions, and drinks with him again when Jude is drowning his sorrows after Sue's marriage to Phillotson, taking him to the popular tavern where he meets Arabella Donn again. Reappears at the drinking party where Jude is made drunk enough to remarry Arabella. *Jude the Obscure*

TAYLORS, the two MISS: They hope to attract the confirmed bachelor Farmer Boldwood, and spend a year upon him, to no avail. *Far from the Madding Crowd*

TEMPETT'S: The best posting house at one end of Sandbourne. Sol Chickerel and Edgar Mountclere hire a coach there while hurrying to prevent Ethelberta Petherwin's marriage to Lord Mountclere. *The Hand of Ethelberta*

TEMPLEMAN, AUNT: Lucetta Le Sueur's rich aunt, whose existence Henchard doubts, but from whom her niece inherits a large fortune, then taking her name. *The Mayor of Casterbridge*

TEMPLEMAN, LUCETTA: A dark-haired, large-eyed, pretty woman of unmistakably French extraction: originally Lucetta Le Sueur of Jersey, she there meets Michael Henchard, flirts with him and, while nursing him through an illness, compromises her reputation. She reproaches him in her fluent love-letters after his return to Casterbridge, but as he has feared, his estranged and long-lost wife Susan is alive and reappears so they cannot marry. Lucetta inherits a handsome fortune from her Aunt Templeman whose name she takes, and moves to Casterbridge intending to restore her good name by marrying Henchard at last, as Susan has meanwhile died. However she falls in love with Henchard's younger enemy, Donald Farfrae, not knowing her friend and companion Henchard's stepdaughter Elizabeth Jane loves him too. Blackmailed by Henchard into an engagement, her inclinations and her prudence, hearing of his youthful rashness, make her secretly marry Farfrae, and though prosperous she is haunted by fear of her former indiscretions, especially her love-letters, becoming known. When this indeed happens, not through Henchard but his unreliable messenger Jopp, local mischief-makers arrange a 'skimmington-ride', a mock pageant ridiculing her, and being then pregnant Lucetta falls into hysterical fits, has a miscarriage and dies. Endowed with natural lightness of heart she has always hoped for the best rather than face up to disagreeable necessities, but her death forestalls her disgrace and Farfrae remembers her with indulgence, if also with some relief. *The Mayor of Casterbridge*

TETUPHANAY, T.: Master of Biblioll College in Christminster, the only college master of the six Jude Fawley writes to who replies to him, though his advice is only to forget learning and stick to his trade. *Jude the Obscure*

THIRDLY, PARSON: Clergyman, not one to wear fine clothes or jewellery, but wins his parishioners' loyalty by unselfish charity. *Far from the Madding Crowd*

THOMAS: One of the Doncastles' menservants, stands in for the butler Chickerel who is overcome by the news of his daughter's marriage to a vicious nobleman. *The Hand of Ethelberta*

One of Paula Power's menservants. *A Laodicean*

THORN, MR.: Solicitor who winds up Ambrose Graye's affairs and agrees to give Cytherea Graye references if necessary. *Desperate Remedies*

'TIME, LITTLE FATHER': Son of Jude and Arabella Fawley, born unknown to Jude eight months after their separation, in Australia. Brought up by Arabella's parents until, being poor, they send him to Arabella now more prosperously settled back in England. Not wanting him, she sends him on to Jude. A small, pale child with large frightened eyes, he is uninterested and unamused by everything in the world and broods on the misfortunes he suffers and sees. He calls Sue Brideshead, with whom Jude is living, his 'mother' but her brightness cannot enliven him, and her periods of depression weigh upon him until, despairing at their poverty and homelessness, he kills Sue's two younger children than hangs himself, leaving a note saying 'Done because we are too menny'. In his octogenarian face is the record of all the brutal coarseness of Jude's first marriage and the super-sensitive suffering of his second. According to the Fawleys' 'advanced' doctor, his precocious awareness is a mark of certain boys in modern society and heralds 'a coming universal wish not to live'. *Jude the Obscure*

TIMMS: A jovial, sharp lawyer, called in for his opinion by

his friend the landlord to the inn where Manston and Cytherea Graye have been told on their wedding night that their marriage is invalid. *Desperate Remedies*

TINKLETON, MR.: A Nonconformist who attends the Imperial Archaeological Association's meeting and has slipped into the fold by chance. *The Hand of Ethelberta*

TIPMAN: Lord Mountclere's trusty valet. He learns from the lady's-maid Menlove, who has discovered it from Joey Chickerel, that Ethelberta Petherwin is the butler Chickerel's daughter. He reveals this to Mountclere who therefore alters his intentions from marriage to seduction of Ethelberta, but pays Tipman and Menlove even more for concealing their discovery when he decides on marrying Ethelberta after all. Tipman's hopes of setting up a shop when he marries Menlove depend on Mountclere's generosity. *The Hand of Ethelberta*

TOMKINS: One of Lord Mountclere's keepers. *The Hand of Ethelberta*

Lives at Norcombe. The rooting up of his great apple tree is reported by Gabriel Oak to his former old neighbour Maltster Smallbury who comments 'stirring times we live in, stirring times'. *Far from the Madding Crowd*

TOPE, ALDERMAN: Walks out into the street to shake hands with John Smith after John's son Stephen becomes distinguished. *A Pair of Blue Eyes*

TORKINGHAM, THE REV.: Clergyman of Welland, a good conscientious clergyman, if unimaginative. He trains the parish choir. *Two on a Tower*

TREMLETT, WILLIAM: A neighbour of Miller Loveday, a member of the local defence force. *The Trumpet Major*

TRENCHER, HOST: Innkeeper of a town near Greenhill who runs a large refreshment booth at the fair. A substantial man of high reputation for catering in all the country round. *Far from the Madding Crowd*

TRENDLE, CONJURER: A celebrated 'conjurer' with power over obstinate butter churns. His son has only a shadow of his power but Dairyman Crick feels obliged to consult him (without actually believing in him) if his milk refuses to turn to butter. *Tess of the D'Urbervilles*

TREWIN, MR. AND MRS.: The bank manager and his wife, who make a point of visiting humble John Smith's garden after John's son Stephen becomes distinguished. *A Pair of Blue Eyes*

TRIBBLE, THOMAS: The smoke across his orchard shows the direction of the wind to the ostler of the Red Lion, Anglebury. *The Hand of Ethelberta*

TRINGHAM, PARSON: An antiquarian of Stagsfoot Lane who first tells John Durbeyfield of his forgotten descent from the noble but decayed D'Urberville family, thus bringing the Durbeyfields disastrously into contact with expectations—and people—above their usual way of life. *Tess of the D'Urbervilles*

TROUTHAM, FARMER: A big man with a red face. His father has been Miss Fawley's father's journeyman and she feels slightly lowered by allowing her little nephew Jude work as rook-scarer for him, the more so when Jude is beaten and dismissed for kindly allowing the rooks a share of the corn—an explanation that doubly infuriates Troutham. *Jude the Obscure*

TROY, EDWARD: A Weatherbury doctor, nominally father of Sergeant Francis Troy, said to be in fact the illegitimate son of a nobleman. *Far from the Madding Crowd*

TROY, SERGEANT FRANCIS (FRANK): Son of a former governess married to a doctor, reputedly illegitimate son of an earl. Throws away a good education by joining the dragoons where he rises to Sergeant. Tall and handsome he is successful with women largely by 'lying like a Cretan', so that when his sweetheart Fanny Robin follows him she finds he was not expecting her, much less preparing for their marriage; and after she brings him up to scratch only to make the fatal mistake of waiting at the wrong church, he evidently forgets about her. His flattery wins the independent Bathsheba Everdene, who marries him, and he leaves the army to live on her farm. His ignorance of farming—which nearly loses their harvest by refusing to believe there will be inconvenient bad weather—and his gambling augur ill for Bathsheba, but disaster strikes him alone when Fanny Robin reappears briefly only to die in childbirth, and Troy, remorseful at last, declares he owes moral allegiance to Fanny, puts up an expensive tombstone for her, and leaves the district. Swept out to sea while swimming, he is reported drowned but in fact works his passage to America on the boat that rescues him, and returns to England much later in a travelling circus where as 'Mr. Francis' he acts Dick Turpin, a showy part that suits him admirably. Recognised by Bathsheba's former dishonest bailiff, he decides to reveal himself, but appearing at the Christmas party he is shot dead by his rival for Bathsheba's hand, Farmer Boldwood. As a man who lives only in the present, Troy passes lightly over the troubles of himself and others; and his first pang of remorse at Fanny's suffering and death passes away until his disruption of Boldwood's life brings its fatal result. *Far from the Madding Crowd*

TROYTON, MRS.: *see* Swancourt, Mrs. Charlotte

TUBBER, ALDERMAN: A jocular and tactless counsellor of Casterbridge, fans Henchard's jealousy of Farfrae. *The Mayor of Casterbridge*

TULLIDGE, CORPORAL: A former soldier, on the shady side of fifty, a watcher at the beacon by night, ready to fire it as a warning of Bonaparte's invasion. Has an old wound in his skull patched with a silver plate, and his arm is crushed into audibly rattling fragments. *The Trumpet Major*

TWILLS, MRS.: She lets lodgings to Fanny Robin who is

following Sergeant Troy's regiment. *Far from the Madding Crowd*

TWILLS, OLD: A farmer who employs old Billy Smallbury only for eleven months at a time to prevent him qualifying for parish relief. *Far from the Madding Crowd*

TYNN, MR. AND MRS.: Member and the member's mainspring for North Wessex. Attend the Imperial Archaeological Association's meeting at Corvsgate Castle. *The Hand of Ethelberta*

U

UNITY: The Swancourts' maid, first generally employed round the house, but after the parson's wealthy marriage she occupies in the new establishment a position between young lady's-maid and middle housemaid. Later marries Martin Cannister on the same day Elfride Swancourt marries Lord Luxellian. *A Pair of Blue Eyes*

UPJOHN, JOHN: A regular worker in Mr. Melbury's timber yard, apparently rather undersized. *The Woodlanders*

UPWAY, GEORGE: A lad of Endelstow village. *A Pair of Blue Eyes*

V

VATT, ALDERMAN: A neighbour of the Farfraes, calls to invite Farfrae to become the next mayor. *The Mayor of Casterbridge*

VENN, DIGGORY: The reddleman, his clothes and skin deeply imbued with the red sheep-marking dye he sells to farmers, though underneath he is evidently handsome and his expression reveals good nature and extreme acuteness. He takes up this wandering outcast's trade when rejected by Thomasin Yeobright, though his father, a prosperous dairy-farmer, has left him a small income. Though he urges Thomasin to marry him instead while Wildeve is procrastinating, he stoically tries to further and protect her marriage, by appealing to her rival Eustacia Vye, and by spying on Wildeve. Coming by chance on the scene of Eustacia's drowning, he pulls out her body and her two would-be rescuers Wildeve and Clym Yeobright. As Wildeve is dead, and Thomasin thus left a widow, Venn gives up the reddle trade, by which he has made enough money to start a large dairy farm, reverts to a normal hue, and marries Thomasin. His exclusion from society has been due to external and temporary disappointments, unlike the disillusionment and tragedy afflicting the solitary Clym Yeobright; and his decisive vigour and opportunism fit him for the social world he re-enters with Thomasin. *The Return of the Native*

VILBERT, PHYSICIAN: A tall, thin, itinerant quack-doctor, a survival from pre-advertising days in that he covers enormous distances on foot peddling his wares himself. He promises to get the boy Jude Fawley Latin and Greek books in return for finding prospective customers, but returns for the customers without bringing the books. Later at an agricultural show, not looking a day older, he sells Arabella Cartlett (*née* Donn) a love potion which later still she uses on him as he attends her next husband, the dying Jude Fawley. When Jude inconveniently dies on a day of festivities, Arabella nevertheless goes out to flirt and see the sights with Vilbert whom she intends for her third husband, as she can't pick and choose as she could when younger. *Jude the Obscure*

VINEY, DAIRYMAN: A respectable Mellstock man, on whom Dick Dewy's wedding procession calls. *Under the Greenwood Tree*

VOSS: Heats the metheglyn and cider for the choir on Christmas Eve and brings these with bread and cheese to the church for midnight refreshment. *Under the Greenwood Tree*

VYE, CAPTAIN: An old man, white as a mountain, bowed in the shoulders and faded in general aspect. Has been in the Royal Navy, as was his father before him, and has a cousin in the peerage. Lives in a remote cottage on Egdon Heath because it is very cheap and has a faint view of the sea, with his granddaughter Eustacia, whom he indifferently leaves free as a bird. *The Return of the Native*

VYE, EUSTACIA: The daughter of a Budmouth lady and a Corfuan musician who takes his wife's name on marrying. When orphaned she has to live with her maternal grandfather on Egdon Heath. Very beautiful with forest-black hair, finely curved lips, and pagan eyes, full of nocturnal mysteries between their heavy lids, she invokes ideas of tropical midnights, rubies and Bourbon roses. She hates Egdon in spite of being preserved by its grandeur from the degrading triviality of her native Budmouth, and longs for grandeur of her own, trying to have a tempestuous love-affair with Damon Wildeve, but he is not great enough for her, and after a quarrel becomes engaged to Thomasin Yeobright. Eustacia, wrongly believing his marriage is delayed for her sake, exerts her charms to win him back, but less interested once he is within her grasp, she turns her attention to the returned heath-dweller Clym Yeobright, rejecting Wildeve. In spite of being 'full-limbed and somewhat heavy' in person, she dresses as a boy-actor in the Christmas mumming play at the Yeobrights', where her femininity is not unnaturally noticed by several, including Clym. Intrigued he seeks her out, they fall in love and marry, against his mother's wishes. Unfortunately her hopes of a glamorous life in Paris are thwarted by Clym's resignation of his job there, and his preparation for setting up a school locally, and when his eyes are weakened by study he contentedly becomes a furze-cutter, alienating her thoroughly. When her mother-in-law Mrs. Yeobright comes to seek reconciliation, Eustacia fails to open the door to her, partly being embarrassed by the presence of Wildeve, partly expecting the sleeping Clym to wake and let his mother in, which he does not. Her failure and Wildeve's visit are reported by a child after Mrs. Yeobright has died of exhaustion while returning from her fruitless journey, causing a violent quarrel and separation between Clym and Eustacia. She decides to go to Paris herself, asks Wildeve to help her, but realises only after setting out that she will have to accept his company as her lover, having no money of her own. Concluding at last that he is still not great enough to dedicate herself to (and perhaps because meanwhile the cottager Susan Nunsuch is destroying an effigy of her), she throws herself into Shadwater Weir. The waiting Wildeve is drowned trying to save her, and Clym and Diggory Venn just escape death in a rescue attempt. Though her potential majesty, courage and ambitions are striking, the massive emptiness of Egdon Heath reduces her aspirations—'How I have tried and tried to be a splendid woman'—in practice to a waiting for splendour to turn up. Depending on opportunity, she superstitiously blames Egdon for thwarting her desires. *The Return of the Native*

W

WARDLAW, MR.: Paula Power's solicitor. *A Laodicean*

WAYWOOD, TED: A member of Dick Dewy's wedding procession. *Under the Greenwood Tree*

WEEDY, GAD: Farmer Springrove's journeyman. *Desperate Remedies*

WERRINGTON: A young man of St. Launce's, who plays and sells musical instruments, a very ringleader of the first class: he only greets John Smith after John's son Stephen becomes distinguished. *A Pair of Blue Eyes*

WESSEX, EARL OF: Great landowner; Geoffrey Day is his keeper in the Mellstock neighbourhood. *Under the Greenwood Tree*

WHITE, MRS.: A customer of the Mellstock butcher Mr. Haylock. *Under the Greenwood Tree*

WHITTLE, ABEL: A round-shouldered, blinking young man of nineteen or twenty, whose mouth falls ajar on the slightest provocation, seemingly because there is no chin to support it. He is an unintentionally persistent late riser, so that his employer Henchard in a fury drags him from bed and sends him out without breeches, which causes the more moderate manager Farfrae's first conflict with Henchard. However when Henchard, a broken and ruined man, spends his last weeks as a field labourer, Whittle, more just and charitable than his former master, accompanies and cares for him, because Henchard 'was kind-like to mother when she were here below, though 'a was rough to me'. *The Mayor of Casterbridge*

WILDEVE, DAMON: Quite a young man, of handsome appearance with a profuse crop of hair, his singular grace in movement being his most fascinating quality. Formerly an engineer, he has declined by reckless living to become landlord of a small tavern, the Quiet Woman, on Egdon Heath. After a quarrel with Eustacia Vye he courts Thomasin Yeobright, and though her mistrustful aunt forbids the banns, their private wedding is next delayed by his own mistake about the licence. Approached meanwhile by Eustacia who wrongly supposes he has delayed for her sake, he begins to court Eustacia again, leaving

Thomasin neither free nor secure. Both he and Eustacia are then piqued to learn that Thomasin may discard him, having another suitor, and as Eustacia also imagines more attractions in the less familiar returning native Clym Yeobright, Wildeve has to make an effort to win back and marry Thomasin. Later his affection for his gentle wife is eclipsed by pity and renewed love for the disappointed Eustacia who wants to escape from her now ailing and unsuccessful husband Clym. He offers to accompany her flight abroad but even the wealth he has unexpectedly inherited can lend him no new glamour, and she drowns herself in Shadwater Weir, where he is drowned too in trying to save her. Moody and sensitive, he values what is unattainable or much sought after, the true mark of the man of sentiment, and his feelings for Thomasin and Eustacia are a subjective mixture of love, sympathy and jealousy: 'He might have been called the Rousseau of Egdon.' *The Return of the Native*

WILDEVE, EUSTACIA CLEMENTINE: Baby daughter of Damon and Thomasin Wildeve, named with unintentional irony after the alienated married Yeobrights, Eustacia and Clement. *The Return of the Native*

WILDEVE, MRS. THOMASIN: *see* Yeobright, Thomasin

WILDWAY, JOHN: An early suitor of Mrs. Penny's, a shoemaker, but they 'have a miff' and part. *Under the Greenwood Tree*

WILKINS, CLERK: His hair-raising accounts of missing bridegrooms are quoted to tease Fancy Day on her wedding day. *Under the Greenwood Tree*

WILKINS, MR.: A rich man who sits down in De Stancy Castle as a guest and rises as its owner. However he becomes blind and never lives there, so it falls into neglect. *A Laodicean*

WILLIAM: A master-mason employed at De Stancy Castle in mediaeval times. *A Laodicean*

One of Lord Mountclere's keepers. *The Hand of Ethelberta*

WILLIAMS, MRS.: A neighbour of Miss Fawley at Marygreen. Having been away, she has to be told the history of Miss Fawley's newly arrived nephew Jude. *Jude the Obscure*

WILLIAMS, PARSON: Parson of Kingsbere church who is amazed at the great musicianship of a visiting player, Yeobright, and wishes for such a man in his parish. *The Return of the Native*

WILLS, BILLY: A glazier, a stout, bucket-headed man who frequents the Three Mariners at Casterbridge. *The Mayor of Casterbridge*

WILTON, PARSON: A former parson of Welland, whose new bride blushes at the wedding psalm sung by his parishioners. *Two on a Tower*

WINTERBORNE, GILES: A deliberate man in the apple and cider trade who also undertakes planting, felling, and other woodland work. He is not very prosperous for his habit of speaking his mind when he speaks at all hinders his trade. Wants to marry his childhood sweetheart Grace Melbury whose father, a very rich wood merchant, wishes to favour Giles for sentimental reasons but also feels Grace by wealth and education deserves a greater match. Giles loses some of his income previously gained by sub-letting cottages when his 'lifehold' lease runs out, and this impoverishment decides Grace's father against him. After an illness his prosperity increases but meanwhile Grace marries Doctor Fitzpiers, though his pride and adultery with Mrs. Charmond make her and her father repent their choice and hope for a divorce to free her to marry Giles. Disappointed in this, Grace still leaves home to avoid her returning penitent husband, and Giles with zealous chivalry gives up his hut to shelter her, sleeping out of doors himself, which brings on the return of his illness. His sacrifice to delicacy costs him his life, and though Grace at first tends his grave she is soon reconciled to her husband, while Marty South,

Giles's companion and fellow-worker in the woodlands, continues to mourn loyally over his sterling, undemonstrative traditional qualities which have been nothing but a hindrance in his unwise aspirations, but which would have made him happy if he had been contented with Marty, his natural counterpart. *The Woodlanders*

WINTERBORNE, JOHN: Giles's father, who, in spite of a great interest in property, dies without extending his family's leasehold of several cottages, as he could legally have done. *The Woodlanders*

WOOD, THOMAS: Formerly a clockmaker of Casterbridge; one of his clocks owned by the Days is familiarly called after its maker. Is taken by Fancy Day when she marries. *Under the Greenwood Tree*

WOODWARD, JOHN: His brother, found drowned and unidentifiable in a Mellstock pond, is recognised as a Woodward by the shoemaker Mr. Penny, by his 'family foot'. *Under the Greenwood Tree*

WOODWELL, MR.: A Baptist minister, an austere man with a smile as pleasant as an infant. He gives away nearly all he has to the poor, tends the sick and teaches the ignorant. Though his outstanding gift is for rhetoric and his sermons outshine all the neighbouring clergy, he usually offends ladies by plain speaking. Singleminded and wholehearted himself, he reprimands the local landowner Paula Power for being as lukewarm as the church of Laodicea. *A Laodicean*

WOOLATT, CHARL: One of Ann Avice Caro's admirers, who will help her with the heaviest laundry work if she lets him. *The Well-Beloved*

WOOLFREY: A Casterbridge draper who sells Union Jacks for the royal visit. *The Mayor of Casterbridge*

WORM, MRS. BARBARA: A wide-faced, comfortable-looking woman with a wart on her cheek. About twice the size of her husband William. *A Pair of Blue Eyes*

WORM, WILLIAM: At first works in Parson Swancourt's house, and is afflicted with a fizzing in his head just like the frying of fish from morning to night. Later becomes a turnpike gatekeeper. *A Pair of Blue Eyes*

WRAY, DR.: Tells Stephen Smith that his constitution will acclimatise well to India. *A Pair of Blue Eyes*

Y

YEOBRIGHT MR.: Father of Thomasin, a man of great indignation against anything underhand, and a masterly musician on both clarinet and bass-viol. Is 'taken bad' at Greenhill Fair, falters on from day to day, then dies in the prime of life. *The Return of the Native*

YEOBRIGHT, MRS.: Aunt of Thomasin, a woman of middle age, her features indicating perspicacity. A curate's daughter, she is a thoughtful, well-educated widow, losing her husband while still young, bringing up alone both her son Clym and orphaned niece Thomasin. Distrusting Thomasin's suitor Wildeve, she publicly forbids the banns of their marriage though later reluctantly consenting. Her ambitions for her son Clym are thwarted not only by his thus not marrying Thomasin but by his abandoning his successful but worldly career with a Paris diamond merchant, and proposing to become a schoolmaster. Her serious principles temper her disappointment a little, but much worse is the blow of his love for the proud, luxurious, indolent Eustacia Vye, and a quarrel soon after their wedding leads to estrangement. Arriving at their cottage to seek reconciliation on a hot day, she is not admitted by Eustacia who is talking to her former lover Wildeve and expects Clym to wake and open the door. However he sleeps on and Mrs. Yeobright, believing both to be deliberately shutting her out, has set off home again before Eustacia at last opens the door. She collapses from the heat and exhaustion, and dies of an adder bite without speaking to Clym who finds her, but the child Johnny Nunsuch reports her last words that she is 'a broken-hearted woman cast off by her son'. Hasty and peremptory in many ways, she is rational and philosophical enough, unlike Eustacia, to come to terms with necessity, though sometimes too late to save suffering. *The Return of the Native*

YEOBRIGHT, CLYM (CLEMENT): A young man of twenty-five whose beautifully-shaped face shows the mark of intense thought, and whose intellect is hampered by his physical needs: his appearance is thus neither wholly handsome nor wholly intellectual, but 'singular'. His early cleverness and artistry lead a local gentleman to assist his widowed mother in educating him, and by chance Clym enters a diamond merchant's in Paris where he rises rapidly, but his philanthropy, ethical reading and intellectual values make him reject this luxury trade to plan a school and a new educational system, for which he returns to his native Egdon Heath and disappointed mother. Here he falls in love with the beautiful, indolent, luxury-loving Eustacia Vye, who hopes to persuade him to return to Paris, and against his mother's wishes they marry. To Eustacia's disgust, he plunges deeper into preparatory study which together with a chill inflames his eyes and almost blinds him. Taking up manual labour, he is quite content to become a furze-cutter. He is sleeping exhausted by labour when his mother calls to seek reconciliation, so he does not open the door to her; nor does Eustacia, who is talking to Wildeve. Clym decides on waking to visit his mother, and finds her collapsed with exhaustion on her way home, where she dies of an adder bite. Upon hearing the report of his mother's last bitterly accusing words, Clym is ill with grief and self-reproach, but later learning of Eustacia's failure to open the door to his mother, he turns his anger upon her, so they quarrel and part. His letter of forgiveness goes astray, and warned by his cousin Thomasin that her husband Wildeve may be eloping with Eustacia, he arrives at Shadwater Weir in time to see Wildeve jumping in after the suicidal Eustacia. Clym is also swept under in trying to save both, and is the only survivor when Diggory Venn rescues all three. Reluctantly remembering his mother's former wish that he should marry Thomasin, he is relieved by her preference for Venn, and devotes his life to becoming a travelling preacher, thus completing the withdrawal from worldly concerns that his marriage has interrupted. A type of modern man for whom thought is a necessity, Clym's intensity of conviction precludes that sense of proportion that would ensure the blessings of happiness and mediocrity. *The Return of the Native*

YEOBRIGHT, MRS. EUSTACIA: *see* Vye, Eustacia

YEOBRIGHT, THOMASIN (TAMSIN): A young woman between pretty and beautiful, with a fair, sweet and honest country face. Darting like a kingfisher, or skimming like a swallow, all similes and allegories concerning her begin and end with birds. She falls in love with the handsome, moody and sensitive Damon Wildeve, but the aunt who has brought her up forbids the banns of their marriage. Thomasin suffers for this when her aunt finally consents, but Wildeve's mistake with the licence delays their wedding, and after a miserable few weeks when she feels neither free nor safely committed, while Wildeve instead of marrying her flirts with her rival Eustacia Vye, she at last, with some disillusion, is married to him. Later Wildeve secretly intends to leave her for Eustacia, providing for her and their baby daughter by giving her half the fortune he has newly inherited, but Thomasin suspects his plan, and begs Eustacia's husband, her cousin Clym Yeobright, to prevent their flight. In fact Eustacia, also disillusioned with Wildeve, drowns herself, Wildeve drowning too in attempting to save her, so that only the need to care for the other rescuers, Clym Yeobright and Diggory Venn, sustains Thomasin against the shock. Left a rich widow, she is consoled eventually by her baby daughter and her naturally hopeful nature, and at last agrees to marry Diggory Venn whom she had rejected many years before. Though sensitive she is a true daughter of Egdon Heath which she respects without superstition: 'Her fears of the place were rational, her dislikes of its worst moods reasonable,' and this strong vein of practicality gives her resilience in the face of tragedy. *The Return of the Native*

YOPPER: An auctioneer, attends Casterbridge market. *The Mayor of Casterbridge*

YORE, DR.: A learned man, who attends the Imperial Archaeological Association's meeting at Corvsgate Castle. *The Hand of Ethelberta*

Animals

BLOSSOM: Miller Loveday's horse. *The Trumpet Major*

Mr. Melbury's skittish mare, which throws and injures the inexpert Dr. Fitzpiers who has mistaken her for the placid mare Darling. *The Woodlanders*

CHAMPION: Festus Derriman's horse, on whose back Anne Garland perilously escapes from his ardent master. *The Trumpet Major*

CRUMPLER: Miller Loveday's cow, whose moo alarms townbred Mathilda Johnson. *The Trumpet Major*

DAINTY: Bathsheba Everdene's horse, which she harnesses to the cart to drive to Bath. *Far from the Madding Crowd*

DAISY: Mrs. Hurst's cow, which Bathsheba Everdene milks. *Far from the Madding Crowd*

DAISY, WHITEFOOT, BONNY-LASS, JOLLY-O, SPOT, TWINKLE-EYE, ETC.: The respectable dairy of Devon cows inherited by Bathsheba Everdene. *Far from the Madding Crowd*

DARLING: The quiet old mare bought by Giles Winterborne to carry Grace Melbury, but sold to her father when Giles's income and hopes of marrying her diminish. *The Woodlanders*

DUMPLING, FANCY, LOFTY MIST, OLD PRETTY, YOUNG PRETTY, TIDY and LOUD: The particular cows at Talbothays dairy which prefer to be milked by Tess Durbeyfield. *Tess of the D'Urbervilles*

GEORGE: Gabriel Oak's wise old sheepdog, accompanies

him to Bathsheba Everdene's farm. *Far from the Madding Crowd*

MOLL: Farmer Boldwood's horse, 'borrowed' by Oak and Coggan to pursue a supposed horse-thief. *Far from the Madding Crowd*

PANSY: Elfride Swancourt's horse. *A Pair of Blue Eyes*

PEGGY: A grizzle horse, time beginning to tell on her, belonging to John Smith. *A Pair of Blue Eyes*

PHENA: One of Mrs. D'Urberville's pet hens. *Tess of the D'Urbervilles*

PLEASANT: An old horse chosen to pull the cart bearing Fanny Robin's coffin. *Far from the Madding Crowd*

POPPET: Bathsheba Everdene's horse, a small animal. *Far from the Madding Crowd*

PRINCE: The Durbeyfields' horse, vital to their business, killed by a mail-cart while Tess is driving him. *Tess of the D'Urbervilles*

SMART: A mare belonging to Reuben Dewy. *Under the Greenwood Tree*

SMILER: A horse belonging to Reuben Dewy. *Under the Greenwood Tree*

STRUT: One of Mrs. D'Urberville's pet cockerels. *Tess of the D'Urbervilles*

TIB: Alec D'Urberville's horse. *Tess of the D'Urbervilles*

TIDY: Farmer Boldwood's horse 'borrowed' by Oak and Coggan to pursue a supposed horse-thief. *Far from the Madding Crowd*

WINKER: A cow. *Tess of the D'Urbervilles*

YOUNG DOG, THE: Son of George, has not yet been named when he stays out all night chasing sheep, sending a flock over a cliff to destruction and ruining his master. Is shot. *Far from the Madding Crowd*

The Characters—Book by Book

Hand of Ethelberta, The

Tess of the D'Urbervilles

Trumpet Major, The

Two on a Tower

Under the Greenwood Tree

Well-Beloved, The

Woodlanders, The